THE NO-BULL GUIDE TO GETTING PUBLISHED AND MAKING IT AS A WRITER

EVERYTHING YOU NEED TO KNOW TO BREAK INTO AND PROSPER IN THIS EXCITING AND LUCRATIVE FIELD

THE NO-BULL GUIDE TO GETTING PUBLISHED AND MAKING IT AS A WRITER

EVERYTHING YOU NEED TO KNOW TO BREAK INTO AND PROSPER IN THIS EXCITING AND LUCRATIVE FIELD

by
MICHELLE WEST

Winslow Publishing

Box 413, Station Z, Toronto, Ontario M5N 2Z5

This edition is a completely revised and expanded edition of a work previously published as *The No-Bull Guide To Getting Published In Magazines And Making It As A Writer,* published by Winslow Publishing, copyright © 1984 by Michelle West.

Cover design by Ric Ward

Typesetting and Printing by Tri-Graphic Printing (Ottawa) Limited

---

Canadian Cataloging in Publication Data
West, Michelle, 1948-

The No-Bull Guide To Getting Published And Making It As A Writer

Earlier editions had title: The No-Bull Guide To Getting Published In Magazines And Making It As A Writer.

ISBN 0-921199-06-6

1. Authorship—Handbooks, manuals, etc.
2. Journalism—Authorship—Handbooks, manuals, etc.

I. Title II. Title: The No-Bull Guide To Getting Published In Magazines And Making It As A Writer.

PN161.W48 1986   808'.02   C86-094431-X

Printed and bound in Canada

This book is dedicated with love to my parents,
Joseph and Evangeline Bucheck,
who never ever let me down,
even when the times were the toughest.

CONTENTS

INTRODUCTION

This is not a very fat book. Chances are, you've already read most of those fat books about writing. And chances are that you're still unpublished, or have only a few things in print.

But you want to write, and get published. And maybe you even have a dream of quitting your regular job and becoming a full-time writer someday. It's a great dream to have, believe me. I had it for many, many years. But it was only when I **stopped** dreaming about making it as a writer and set forth on a systematic plan for achieving that goal, did I succeed.

We are living in an age of extraordinary plenty. If you are a writer, there are more magazines to write for now than at any other time in history. Old magazines are getting fatter and new magazines are appearing each and every month.

The scope of this can be understood if you simply study the racks at your local magazine store. As you know, those racks used to display magazines head-on, so that you could see the whole cover. But these days there are so many magazines that they have to overlap them—so that you can only see an inch or two of the spine—and you really have to dig to find the one you want. And that is wonderful! The more magazines there are, the more opportunities there are for writers.

But there are also more writers than ever before. In fact, almost everybody I know does a little writing or would like to. When you succeed, most of your friends will envy you, if they say anything or not. Most people would give anything to be able to consistently have things published—so that they can either quit their jobs and just write, or just bring in a little extra money.

In fact, if you ask any 100 people you will probably find that at least 90% of them already have some stories or poems they've written hidden in a drawer or shoebox somewhere. I'm not sure exactly why so many people have such a desire to write—it goes far beyond just seeing one's name in print in a magazine (although this is an incomparable high). It is more like that writing gives every one of us a chance to tell other people, in a lasting form (a printed page), our hopes and ideas. A bit of immortality, if you will.

But this brings up a good question. Can you really succeed when there is so much competition? That depends on you, and on how much you **want** to succeed. Many people have vague dreams of "becoming a writer" someday, but it is only when you have a definite plan—and follow it through—that you can begin to make it.

You will find that, no matter how much competition there is out there, many editors are always frantically searching for new writers. Study several issues of any magazine and you'll see that they always use the same writers over and over again—why do you think that is so? Well, it is simply because the editors know that they can always count on those few writers —really truly count on them.

But a good editor also knows that his magazine isn't everything that it could be if he keeps using the same writers all the time. New blood, new perspective, is vital to a magazine's continuing success.

So why are editors having such a tough time finding new writers, when almost everybody wants to be a writer?

The answer to this question is complex, but primarily boils down to the fact that a goodly number of the new writers are not willing to "follow the rules". (Yes, Virginia, just like in the rest of the world, there are rules!) Many people get lost along the way simply because they are bad writers —and aren't willing to learn to be better—but even more do not get the chance they deserve because they just don't understand how things work, just don't understand the "system".

Anyone who says that there isn't freelance writing work out there simply is not really looking, or else not going about it properly. There are more magazines than ever before, and most magazines are getting more advertising because the economy is in good shape. And editors have to balance out all of that advertising with articles. Never has there been a better time for someone just starting out.

This book is not about how to write. There are many excellent books out there about the form and style of writing, and I encourage you to read some of them. But this book is about **selling** what you write. Because we all know that there is a world of difference between writing and writing for money.

Now there is nothing wrong with writing for its own sake. In fact, just the opposite. It's rewarding, fun, therapeutic, and may even make you famous in some way or another someday. On top of that, any writing makes you a better writer. If you want to sit home and write, go for it.

I have a close friend who spent seven years writing a novel. It is over 1,700 typed pages long, and although it is a fascinating story, would never in a million years get published. He enjoyed writing this book, and I'm very proud of what he has accomplished—but I refuse to listen to him when he complains that he can't get the book published. (One publisher actually read this massive novel, and said that she'd look at it again if the author would cut it by perhaps two-thirds . . .)

They say that if you give the people what they want you will be successful. That has been my credo since I started taking my writing seriously. Write what people **want** to read, what magazines **want** to publish, and do it reasonably well, and you will sell your work. It is really that simple.

Many more magazines than you might think are actually crying out for good writers that they can really depend on. (And more than one magazine has folded because they really couldn't find any.) And there are a lot of excellent writers out there who just can't hook up with a magazine that really needs them, simply because they don't know the rules—or because they think they're so great that they don't have to follow them. A few people do get away with it for a while, but most don't. Almost any editor will tell you that he would much rather have a reasonably good writer who is dependable and honest and who cares than one who is brilliant and doesn't. And that is the truth. And that is what this book is all about.

If someone presented you with a system that would guarantee that you would absolutely win the next time you went to Las Vegas, it would be a waste if you read it but still kept on playing (and losing) the same old way you always did before. That is, if you really want to win. Some people like losing, you know.

3

And I've found that some people **like** not being published. It gives them something to talk about, something to complain about—a good reason to seek sympathy. They want to suffer! You know that old stuff—that you have to paper your walls with rejection slips before you'll be considered to have suffered enough and can then become successful. Nonsense! There are really only two reasons why so many really great writers had such a rough time of it many years ago—there simply weren't many magazines around, and they didn't know the marketing skills necessary to sell themselves and their work.

When you really deep-down-in-your-soul decide that you want to be a successful writer, and make good money that way, you can do it. You'll need a few things, but you can do it if you really want to. First, you'll need to learn to write reasonably well, through books, classes or just practice—good writers are **made,** not born—anyone can learn to write better if he or she really wants to.

Second, you'll need some money to tide you over until you can establish yourself. How long this will take depends on many things. But it's really hard to find enough quality time to write while you're working a full-time job. Perhaps you could try working only part-time, or working for a while and saving every penny so you can take a few months off, or taking out a loan, or taking in a roommate. (Or you can do what I did—live on your charge cards!)

The third thing you need is to learn the rules. That's the easy part, because you're holding them right in your hands. Read them a couple of times if you can—this skinny book only takes two or three hours to read. And even more importantly, follow my suggestions. Like the system for winning in Vegas, it won't work if you don't use it. If you really want to make it as a successful writer you'll have to start doing things this way eventually anyway—and believe me, it's easier to make it easy on yourself right from the beginning.

This book contains no bull. Believe everything here, because this is the way things really are.

WHO AM I
TO BE WRITING THIS BOOK?

I am a professional writer, and I am very proud to say that. Most people mean two different things by the word "professional" in this context. First, it means that you make your entire living that way. And second, it means that you have achieved and maintained certain high standards of excellence in your work. I am very proud of both.

I started writing while in high school. I wrote hundreds, perhaps thousands, of short stories, poems and articles. I sent countless manuscripts to countless teen and confession magazines. I wrote my first novel at 15. I still have many of these things—and they're not too bad. A little childish, a little misdirected, but not bad. I lived in a small town and never had the opportunity to talk with a real writer. And in the mid-1960's there weren't any books about marketing yourself and your work.

But even if there had been, I probably wouldn't have followed their advice. Writers are artists of a sort, you know, and art doesn't always listen to reason. It took me literally **years** to really figure out how everything really worked, and how I should be working.

Unfortunately, a lot of very good and talented people give up—or are forced to give up—before they figure it all out!

My Father worked regular hours and my Mother worked nights while I was in high school. My Mother would pick me up from school and then go to work, so I had a couple of free quiet hours all to myself before my Father came home each evening. This is when I wrote, typing on the dining room table on the old Smith-Corona my brother left behind when he went off to college.

I wrote about things that I was interested in at the time—generally things I had no real experience with. I wrote teenage love/confession stories before I had ever been kissed. I wrote a lot about boys and cars and even auto racing. (Lots of Indiana kids are interested in auto racing.)

As soon as I would finish a story, I'd wrap it up and ship it off to one of the magazines I read and loved—Seventeen, True Story, Glamour, Teen, etc. I never told my parents that I was doing this, as I wanted to surprise them when I had something accepted.

Every New Year's Eve the very first thing on my list of resolutions was to "get something published this year".

I kept writing all through high school, and sending out manuscripts, and getting rejection slips. Once I got a personal note at the bottom of one of these rejection slips from Glamour. It was very simple—"keep trying" or some such thing—but it brightened my spirits and kept me going for months afterwards.

I started sending things out like that in 1962—and never ever got **anything** published that way!

When I went off to university I was too busy to do much creative writing, although my stories required for composition class won me the Bradley University Freshman Writing Award in 1967. Once graduated and working, I tried to find time to do some writing again. But I did the same exact things I did earlier—writing mainly short stories and poems and sending them out unsolicited. Again, nobody ever wanted anything I sent them.

I had my first article published in 1972, in a small magazine for no pay. (I had written scores of things for both my high school and university newspapers and literary magazines, but although this made for excellent experience and practice, it didn't quite "count" as far as I was concerned. Only getting published in a real bound magazine was "getting published", the fulfillment of my many New Year's Resolutions.)

I was quite involved in intercollegiate chess when I was in university and for a few years after, and in 1972 I asked a friend of mine who was the editor of a chess magazine if he wanted a write-up of a tournament I was attending. (My first query!) He did, and I was published. I bought about thirty copies and sent them to all of my friends! It was unbelievably exciting for me, after so many years of struggle. And it inspired me to no end.

In 1973 I got my first check from a magazine that paid for "letters to the editor". I wanted to keep it, frame it, but I needed the fifty bucks! I did, however, make several photocopies of it before I cashed it.

In 1976 I got my first real paying assignment—a cooking column in a small new magazine—$16 a month! I was reading one of those "buy and sell" type newspapers while working at a boring job to pay the rent while I was trying to establish myself as a writer, and I noticed an ad for this new magazine for singles. I figured that I had nothing to lose by calling them, and it turned out that they were thrilled to hear from me. The magazine was being run and totally written by men, and none of them had even considered putting a cooking column in the magazine. So I had a "writing job". I wrote my little column for that magazine until it folded about a year later.

In 1979 I got my first "big break". I stumbled upon another brand new magazine—also for singles, it so happened—this time by reading an ad for it in the "Personals" column of the Saturday newspaper. They paid very little and were in desperate need of writers. I met with the editor and was able to convince him that I was a really good writer and could write "anything".

So I wrote for him. He needed a lot of stuff, and almost anything I suggested he went for. Some weeks I wrote practically the whole magazine, using up to seven different names. This magazine folded after about 30 weekly issues, but by then I had had more than 100 articles published. And even though the magazine didn't make it, I wrote some darn good stuff for them!

I took the best of these articles and had good photocopies made—and they opened the doors to bigger and better things for me.

Sure, I had been "writing" during all those years between high school and that big break—at age 31! Writing a lot. And sending manuscripts out, hither and yon. And getting them back. ("Thank you for thinking of us, but this just doesn't suit our needs at this time, sweetie.") I started doing that in 1962—and I never got **anything** published that way!

Like many people, for years I spoke beautiful dreams of "becoming a writer". But it wasn't until 1980 that I really decided that that was what I wanted to do. I mean really really-deep-down-in-my-soul decided.

The taste of writing for that weekly magazine was heaven. Because it was a weekly, and because I wrote so much stuff, I made enough money at seven cents a word to squeak by, and I didn't have to work at another job. I was heartsick when that magazine folded.

But just around that same time I read a book that changed my life, and I would like to encourage you to read it too. It will give you courage. It's called *Feel Free* by Dr. David Viscott. It's never come out in paperback that I know of, so you'll have to try to find one in your local library. Believe me, it's worth the hunt.

This book is about deciding what you really want to do with your life, what you **must** do, to make you happy. But it not only helps you decide, it helps you form a plan of action to go after what you want, no matter how impossible your circumstances may be or seem to be.

After reading this book I knew that nothing else in the world could possibly satisfy me—I had to be a writer. I was sick of working a regular job and trying to squeeze my writing in on weekends. (You cannot possibly do your best work that way.) It had to be all or nothing for me.

I knew that I had the talent, and this book gave me the courage. I decided to give it an honest try—like it explains in the book—and if I didn't make it, I wouldn't have lost anything. At least I'd never have to look back and say "What if . . ."

So I spent a lot of time analyzing my situation. Having never even gotten one thing published in 18 years of sending out unsolicited manuscripts, it finally dawned on me that maybe I should follow the advice in some of those writing books I'd been reading and start sending out query letters instead. Having never even gotten a nod of approval from any magazine even approaching national status (hereafter known as the "biggies"), and having had great luck with two brand new and very appreciative magazines, I decided to follow my head for once and stick with the little magazines until I had more good credits and could go after the bigger ones.

NOBODY COULD HAVE TOLD ME THESE THINGS BEFORE . . .
I had to learn everything the hard way.

But, geesh, when you're 16—20—even 30—and a dreamer, who can tell you anything?

Once I made these incredible discoveries, I embarked on a systematic plan of action. I made goals, I worked towards them step-by-step, and now—in only about six years—I am a very successful and established professional writer who is writing this book to celebrate my 350th published article!

Sure, many of those articles were small, but I got paid for every one of them (except that first one), and in some cases got paid very well. Since I started out in small new publications, most of the first magazines I wrote for have bit the dust. It's a very competitive business. (If you think it's tough being a writer, you should try being a publisher!) But it doesn't matter. I wrote some very good stuff for them—I never let the size of the magazine influence how much I put into an article—and even though the magazines have not made it, I have multitudes of tearsheets that have opened fabulous doors for me. Now I feel confident to approach any biggie, and know that they will at least talk to me. I still haven't been able to land assignments from Good Housekeeping or Cosmopolitan (my own personal "Holy Grail"), but at least they speak to me—and nicely, I may add.

In early 1985 I was offered the job of editor for a small new trade magazine. It is an experience I recommend for any writer. Just being "on the other side of the desk", as they say, was a real eye opener. It has enabled me to write a lot of things in this new revised edition of this book that I could not have written in the first edition—because I did not know.

I absolutely loved being an editor. Although I put in almost as many hours as I did when I was writing full-time, I actually found it much less stressful—but then, it was a very small magazine. Unfortunately the magazine was sold to new people after about ten months and I lost my job because they wanted to do everything themselves.

I actually had **two** "big breaks" in my writing career. The first was recounted above—the second one I made for myself. I want to tell you about it because there is no reason in the world why you cannot do exactly the same thing. In fact, you can probably do it even better and faster than I did, because I'll tell you how.

Between 1980 and the end of 1982 I did okay with my writing. I was writing for six magazines regularly, one of which loved me so much that I wrote four columns and up to four features for each issue. Unfortunately it only came out four or five times a year. (It was supposed to be a bi-monthly, but the publisher frequently had a little trouble getting the issues out.)

I was not quite making enough money to live, and was constantly taking advances on my charge cards to pay the rent. On New Year's Eve of 1983 I sat down to have another long talk with myself.

There was no doubt that I loved writing and that I was doing pretty well with it. But I was tired of being broke. I had been sending out occasional queries, but hadn't had much luck. How could I change this? Well, the answer became obvious to me—I could start sending out more queries.

So starting with the first week of 1983, I made myself send out one query every week—to somebody, anybody. It took a while to get the ball rolling, but eventually I started getting some answers. But rain or shine I sent out a query every Monday morning. As the weeks went by I even became very very bold, sending queries to some of the biggest magazines, like TV Guide and Good Housekeeping. I had some wonderful tearsheets, so why not?

Almost nothing happened until June—and then everybody on earth started calling me. Was every other writer on vacation in the Bahamas?

I got so many assignments during the summer months that I actually had to stop sending out queries.

I had 10 articles due in September, 18 in October, 22 in November. (I took December off.) Needless to say, I absolutely wore myself out— but paid off all my charge cards!

Most of the new (to me) magazines I made contact with during that period liked my first assignments and gave me more work. I even got three contracts from TV Guide. Those queries I sent out paid off for years.

I would like to suggest that as soon as you finish reading this book (and perhaps read the chapters on queries twice), you start doing the same thing. Even if you've never had anything published. Go to a library or magazine store and find a few small magazines you'd like to write for, get your stationery printed up, and go for it.

If you're very anxious to see some results in your writing career, send out two or three queries a week instead of just one. There are so many magazines out there now, and they all need writers. But they won't come to you—they don't even know you exist. You have to spread the word about yourself.

Keep up with your resolution to send out a lot of good and perfect queries regularly—it cannot help but pay off. If you are seeing no results, try reading the chapters on queries again—you may have missed something. But unless you are sending queries to magazines that are totally out of your league, or sending out queries with errors or inappropriate ideas, you should start getting assignments in no time at all.

I do not believe that you must "paper your walls with rejection slips" before you can succeed at writing. In fact, I think you should burn all of the rejections slips you may have. If you keep them around they will only bring you down. If you follow everything in this book, you will be published soon.

There have never been as many opportunities as there are right this very minute. Go confidently ahead, and you'll make it!

I'M A WORKING WRITER,
HOW ABOUT YOU?

Most kinds of writing are simply work. It's a job, just like sweeping the streets or running a big corporation. Anybody who tells you that it isn't work is not really telling the truth. While fiction may be easier than non-fiction for some people, you still have to do research, etc. Novels these days are tremendously complicated, covering different eras, political climates and locations, and having dozens of intricate, deep characters. Facts must be accurate, and this takes a lot of study.

Non-fiction can sometimes be sheer slave labor. Dozens of interviews, hours of research, checking and rechecking of facts, not to mention writing and rewriting—most of which must of necessity be done on a solitary basis. On the whole, writing for a living is not the glamorous life many people believe it is. Only those who write best-selling books seem to get that glamour.

Ah, but I didn't say it wasn't exciting! Seeing your name in print is a real high. Seeing it in print in a large national glossy magazine is even better. When you first go to the newsstand to check out the new issue to see if your article is really there, like the editor told you it would be, you literally want to scream out to everybody else in the store: "LOOK! I WROTE THIS!" And so it is this recognition that most writers strive for in lieu of the glamour.

But even though writing is hard work, I wouldn't do anything else. The hours are fabulous. I can choose my working environment and control almost everything. It's fun hearing kids and regular people say WOW! when you tell them what you do for a living. I love it when people pull me aside at parties and ask me how to get started. (And that's why I wrote this book!)

And I don't want to forget to say this—if you write a lot, and for the right magazines, the pay can be very good indeed.

Now don't misunderstand. Although writing gives me more freedom than almost any other job, I still do have to work. I still have deadlines, and I still have occasional times when I'm up all night the night before something is due—typing. So while you're free to control your life yourself, it is within limits—because you still do have to write what you're supposed to write. Good time management skills are vital to a working writer if everything is to get done on schedule. After we write best-sellers and make a million dollars, only then can we write what and when we want. (Personally, I'm still anxiously waiting for that to happen!)

If you want to make a decent living—say over $20,000 a year—that generally takes a lot of articles. Very few magazines can afford to pay $1000 for an article, although some, like Reader's Digest, pay even more. (But then again, it may take you two months to write a $3000 article for Reader's Digest.) Most magazines that would really give a break to a beginner will pay much less. I consider $500 to be very good pay for an article of reasonable length. Once you start making that kind of money regularly, you're in the big leagues.

I got $50 for my first paid published article, but I've written many that got less than that. But I feel that it does work out in the end. Low-paying articles are easier to write and take less time—so you can write a lot more of them. Quantity will have to make up for high pay.

So if you want to write for a living, to make enough money to support yourself, you have to be prepared to work. There's no time to wait for the right "mood", or to wait until the muse inspires you. This is a luxury allowed only to those who are rich enough to write only when they want to. Editors won't accept excuses like that. If you have seven articles due at the end of the month, you have seven articles due at the end of the month. Period. There's no time for "writer's block". You have to learn to budget your time so that everything gets done.

If you want to make a good living, it will probably take at least 40 hours a week, and occasionally more. It would be nice if all articles paid $2000 each so that we only had to do one a month and could take the rest of the time off—but it doesn't work that way. When you have nothing to do, and even when you're your busiest, you still have to constantly keep hustling for work so that you'll have something to do next month. It never stops.

Writing novels may be more leisurely (assuming some anxious publisher hasn't given you a tight deadline for the manuscript). You may only have to do a novel every year, or even every other year, to keep the bills paid. But making a living at writing non-fiction for magazines is a constant activity.

If you're like me, you'll probably find yourself unable to stop thinking about your current project at times. Our work is different from other kinds in that we are never really away from it. Most other workers leave their factory or office at 5:00 and never give their job a second thought until they go back to work the next morning. They are totally free to do and think about other things all night.

But a writer always has something in the typewriter. Once you start getting regular work from magazines, you'll have times when you don't know which article to think about first. You'll find that you get to a point where almost everything you see or hear triggers an idea in your mind, and you'll rummage through your purse or pocket for your notebook right in the middle of a good conversation with friends or spouse.

Don't worry about it—your friends will understand. (They may think you're a little eccentric, but they'll understand. Writers have always been considered a little eccentric.) Just be sure that you do always have a notebook with you, because ideas are frequently just wisps. If you don't grab them right away, they're gone.

Of prime importance is keeping a notebook by your bed. I get most of my very best ideas right before falling asleep, and you probably will too. Don't neglect to write them down immediately, for they'll be gone in the morning.

But please remember one thing. When you're going crazy because you have seven articles due at the end of the month, and don't even know where to start—remember this day, today. Remember all the times you were so disappointed when you got a rejection slip. You thought that maybe you'd never get published.

You can be very, very proud of yourself once you start raking in multiple assignments, because you will have made it through your own hard work. This is one field of endeavor where good work is really recognized and applauded. You may be handed an assignment on a silver platter by a relative or something—but if you don't do good work, your article will never see print.

If you always work hard and do your best, you can't help but succeed!

SLOW AND STEADY VS. INSTANT GRATIFICATION

I have a friend who sold the very first article she ever wrote to Cosmopolitan. I'm sure that you've heard of people who have had that sort of extraordinary luck. But believe me, that is truly the exception to the rule.

I met a girl at a party once, and she took me aside when she learned I was a magazine writer. She really started bending my ear. I thought she wanted some tips on how to get published, but I was wrong. She just wanted someone to dump on.

She spoke for a long time about how "most" editors don't even bother to answer her queries, even though she always sends an SASE (self-addressed stamped envelope). "I thought that they needed good writers," she said, exasperated. I asked her which magazines she had been getting such shoddy treatment from.

"Oh," she replied, "all the magazines that you'd think would treat people better—Playboy, Redbook, Connoisseur . . ." I stopped her in midsentence.

"How many articles did you say you've had published?" I asked her.

"None yet—how can I possibly get anything published if they won't even answer my letters?!"

I tried to explain the facts of writing to her, but I don't think she listened. When I was young I probably wouldn't have listened to anyone either.

For the longest time, I felt that there would be one, and only one, "great" thing that I could do that would firmly establish me as a writer—if only I could just find it! One absolutely fabulous article, one best-selling novel. And poof! I'd really be a writer.

I'm older now, and much wiser. And after you finish reading this book, you will be too.

People who have grown up in the past 30 years or so are different from those who are older. Those of us born after the Second World War were always indulged a little. We always had almost everything we wanted, and if we couldn't afford it, we "charged it". It is called "Instant Gratification", always getting exactly what we want immediately when we want it, and many people truly believe that the whole world works that way.

Well, I'm sorry to have to be the one to tell you, but writing is not like that. Sure, once in a while it happens—a housewife who has never before put pen to paper occasionally writes a best-selling novel and makes a million dollars the first time out. But for most people, life doesn't work that way.

Of course, it is a lovely dream to have—but it almost never happens. If you are the kind of person who cannot wait for things, who must see immediate results (and immediate rewards) at all times, then you shouldn't plan on being a writer, for life will be nothing but frustration for you.

Because for every writer who sells her first article to Cosmopolitan, for every writer whose first novel becomes a best-seller, there are hundreds of thousands of working writers who toil unfamous and practically un-rewarded, maybe for their whole lives.

Most successful writers start small, working for low pay for small magazines. Then when they have enough good tearsheets (copies of things they have already had published), they approach bigger magazines. And if they turn in consistently good and competent work, the magazines which request their services get bigger as time goes by. (This is the clichéd equivalent of "starting in the mail room" and then eventually becoming the president of the company. It's an old tried-and-true method for success. And nowhere does it work better than in the magazine world.)

Actually, making it as a writer is not difficult at all. It takes a reasonable amount of hard work—maybe for years—but it's quite a simple step-by-step procedure. If you're unwilling or unable to work that way, perhaps you should consider some other line of work.

They say that if you give the people what they want, you will be successful. Write what people want to read, what magazines want to publish, and do it reasonably well, and you will sell your work. It is really that simple.

That young writer I spoke with at that party is wasting a lot of time writing things that nobody cares to look at, and sending out queries that are immediately filed in the circular file. If she feels that she is "too good" a writer, and has "too great" ideas to waste on smaller, lesser publications, she may never get published, and I told her this. She is simply aiming too high—too far out of her league—at this point of her career.

But this is basically the same thing I was doing when I started out—of course, to a lesser degree. Teen and True Story are hardly the same caliber as Playboy and Connoisseur. But it's the same idea. You're probably doing it too. It's a real coup to get in a glossy national biggie, and every writer probably dreams of making his or her first sale in such a spectacular fashion. But seriously folks, if you would really like to become a professional writer, or even just one who gets a couple of regular assignments a month, you'll have to "start out in the mail room" if you like that idea or not. If you insist that only sales to a biggie will satisfy you, and you never even contact any smaller publications, then you are probably not serious enough about being a working writer.

Now I'm not saying that we shouldn't have dreams! I'm still dreaming of being in Cosmopolitan one day. Dreams keep us going when times are tough. By all means dream—but at the same time work hard at something that will produce results that will help to fulfill those dreams!

But if you insist on making Cosmo the first time out, you're in for a very bumpy ride. You'll also probably never make it as a writer unless you change your thinking. For there is no regular dependable magic in the publishing world. Sure, you may very well be fortunate enough to have the perfect idea at the perfect place at the perfect time, and get one of your first articles into a biggie—but a feat like that is almost impossible to duplicate regularly enough to make a decent living until you've been established for a long time.

Slow and steady is the only way you'll really make it.

IF YOU'RE UNPUBLISHED, THERE'S A REASON

I'd like to say that again. If you're unpublished, or seldom-published, there **is** a reason. You may have never thought about it quite that way, but it's true. Coldly true. And editors know it. Believe me, they know it.

Now, the reasons for not being published may be very simple and straightforward. Perhaps you write something very specialized, and just haven't been able to connect with a market yet. Or perhaps you spend too much time writing and not enough time trying to find homes for what you produce. Or maybe you're too easily discouraged, and will not send out an idea for an article more than two or three times. Maybe you're only trying to get published in magazines that are way out of your league. Or maybe you just haven't had the luck to meet up with someone who recognizes your obvious talent and/or appreciates you.

These things can all be overcome reasonably easily.

But there are **other** reasons why you may have remained virtually unpublished, and the editors know all about these. And since they don't know you personally, they consequently don't know exactly why you haven't appeared in print. It might be just too much of a chance for them to trust you with an assignment, even a small one, until they see that you've come through for someone else. For these "other reasons" can upset their schedules and cost them time and money.

You may be unpublished because you cannot come up with good and appropriate ideas, because you cannot follow through on the ideas you do come up with, because you do not listen to what the editors want and always do your articles the wrong way, because you cannot complete articles by the deadlines, or because you may simply be a royal pain to work with. An editor will almost always choose an experienced, proven writer over an unproven one. He cannot afford to take the chance to do otherwise.

Every editor has literally hundreds of horror stories about unreliable, crazy, egotistical, sloppy, and/or simply bad writers. A lot of people sincerely want to be published and make it as a writer, and will always do their very best—but a lot of people are simply not capable of doing the job.

So when you ask an editor who doesn't know you for an assignment, and he sees that you haven't had anything published, it starts him wondering. Why? He knows the many things you could be doing badly or wrong. And the more bad experiences he has had with **other** people, the less he may be willing to take a chance on you. (Sad, but unfortunately true.)

Put yourself in his shoes for a moment. Two writers come to you with the same good idea at the same time. It's a big important article, maybe even the cover story. One writer has had 34 articles published, and the other has none. Which one would you choose? The former has proven to someone—at least 34 times—that she is reliable and can handle the job. The latter is an unknown quantity. If the article is important (and most editors think that absolutely every article is important), he will probably choose the known, proven writer.

So now we are presented here with that age-old question: "If I need experience to get the job, and nobody will give me a shot, how am I supposed to get the experience?"

And that is exactly what this skinny book is about. Don't forget that everybody has to start somewhere. That was true 40 years ago, and it's still true today. If you're still in high school, or if you're 68 years old with time on your hands, no matter. There **is** a way to get started!

WHAT TO WRITE

Since I've promised you that this book will contain no bull, I'll be honest. If you want to write short fiction and poetry, you're going to have a rough time getting published. Everybody starts out writing short fiction and/or poetry, so there is a lot more competition. And there are fewer magazines all the time that are even interested in printing this kind of writing for pay.

If you look through the *Fiction Writer's Market,* a nice fat book, you'll see that there are indeed plenty of markets—but many if not most of them pay little if at all, or just pay in copies of the magazine. This is okay, of course, if you don't care about the money. But by now you know the difference between writing and writing for money, and if you bought this book, you're probably interested in making some money with your writing—perhaps even enough to enable you to write full-time.

Now there are some people who do make very nice livings writing short fiction exclusively—I just want to warn you that it will be a long and hard road. The magazines that do publish a lot of fiction are frequently poor and cannot pay well. And you'll have an inordinant amount of competition for those few pages.

You also have to be prepared to waste a lot of time that you may not need to if you write fiction, because you have to write the whole story first and then try to sell it. (With non-fiction, if nobody wants to buy your article after reading your query, you don't have to write the article.) Few editors will be able to make a decision about a fiction piece from a query letter, because fiction is something that must be read to be evaluated. Even the most dynamite idea may be difficult or impossible to execute.

So with fiction you almost have to go the "unsolicited manuscript" route, sending your story to editor after editor until someone bites. And in addition to the time spent writing individual covering letters and sending your manuscripts around, and time delays while waiting to hear from each editor, you also spend a lot of extra money—all that postage, the envelopes and photocopies.

Most fiction book publishers will gladly accept a couple of sample chapters and a detailed outline of the rest of your novel, but if you're an unknown, chances are that you'll still have to complete the book before you could talk them into giving you a contract to publish the book. However, this may be a blessing in disguise, as it can save you a lot of time. If you send sample chapters around to a dozen publishers, and they all tell you that your sample (or the idea for the book) stinks, at least you'll be saved the time of finishing it.

If you write **really** good short fiction and send it around a lot, you'll probably hit the jackpot somewhere without too much trouble. Most unsolicited fiction manuscripts are thrown onto a pile containing hundreds (or perhaps even thousands) of similar pieces—because almost everybody writes short fiction when they're starting out, and because everybody seems to send their stuff to the same magazines. This is known as the "slush pile", and your poor manuscript may be indeed doomed if it is not truly outstanding.

In many cases a junior editor or proofreader (or even secretary or filing clerk) will read your story first, passing it up the ladder to someone who could make a decision about it only if he or she feels it has merit. The problem with this system is that the person who first reads your story may simply not appreciate the kind of fiction you write or may not even have any taste.

With magazines that do publish a lot of fiction, like the confession, mystery, science fiction and literary-type magazines, your treatment will be much better. You'll be read by someone who really cares and is really scouting that slush pile, hoping to uncover a real gem of a talent. Remember that the sales (and advertising sales) of this type of magazine are tied totally into the editors finding great fiction to print, unlike primarily non-fiction magazines. So they are anxious to get to know you if you're good.

However, as a rule, these magazines do not pay as well as non-fiction magazines. In fact, some of the literary-type magazines do not pay at all, or pay only in subscriptions or copies of the issue containing your article. Many struggle for their very lives.

But again, some people do make nice livings writing short fiction. Because of the higher degree of competition, you'll have to write extraordinarily well and have outstanding story lines so that you'll stand out from the crowd. With fiction, the writing itself is much more important than with non-fiction, so be sure that you're well-versed in construction, plot, character development and so on. There are many excellent books about writing fiction; you'll probably need them all to give you an edge.

If you write fiction, the most important book in your library should be the *Fiction Writer's Market,* which is published by Writer's Digest Books each year. This book is absolutely invaluable—be sure that you have the most recent copy and read it from cover to cover.

If you're interested primarily in writing poetry, it's basically the same story. Almost everybody writes poetry, and it really seems like they all send their poems to the same places. But even the slickest non-fiction magazines do need some poetry—if for no other reason than to fill up little spaces left over when articles run a couple of inches short. And some, like Cosmopolitan, Cat Fancy and Essence, frequently run pages or half-pages of poems on a theme. I've never tried to get a poem published, but I am sure that any magazine looking for a few poems would be much more interested in the quality of your pieces rather than in your publication credits. And you will have to be very good—everybody thinks they write great poetry, and magazine editors seeking two good poems may have to wade through six thousand to find them. A great letterhead and great typing will certainly not hurt your cause.

If you are serious about getting poems published, I suggest that you read several of the poetry magazines and join some of the poetry groups that advertise in them. You'll hear about good markets through them. Writer's Digest Books also publishes a *Poet's Market.* If you do very good work, you should not have too much trouble getting published. Magazines that publish a lot of poetry are always looking for really good stuff.

When you look for well-paying markets, however, it is obvious that most magazines today are primarily or exclusively non-fiction. That means that there are considerably more opportunities for non-fiction writers. And most new magazines being started up at this time are exclusively non-fiction, simply because the publishers want to make money. There's not that much money in fiction magazines—that's why they're frequently printed on cheap paper and sometimes don't pay for manuscripts. Some of them do very well, but are nothing compared to the slick national glossies like Playboy, Cosmopolitan, Good Housekeeping or Connoisseur.

Just spend a couple of hours browsing through your copy of the *Writer's Market* or *The Writer's Handbook* some afternoon. It's painfully obvious where the good money is. And it's even more obvious where most of the opportunities are.

If you want to write fiction, by all means write fiction. Please don't misunderstand me on this. There is nothing wrong with writing fiction. It's a valuable contribution to the world, and if you're really good, it will be you who becomes that millionaire best-selling author. But if your goal is to make a living writing short fiction, you'll have a rough time of it. You will find it many times easier to make good money writing non-fiction unless you're truly outstanding.

When starting your non-fiction writing career it's not a bad idea to specialize. If you know a lot about anything—gardening, pets, cooking, space exploration, motherhood, computers, etc.—you may find it easier to make repeated sales in that area. You can always branch out later.

Of course, you don't really need to know anything about a subject to specialize in it. Just select something that really interests you. Be sure that it really interests you or you may quickly become sick of it.

Once you've picked an area to specialize in, all you really need to find out is where to look for your research tools and whom to ask your questions of, and you can write absolutely anything. Even if you don't know anything about it!

I'm a specialist in home video now—but in 1981 when I stumbled upon the opportunity to write for a glossy national video magazine I knew nothing except how to work the controls on my own VCR. But I was confident of my ability to find the right questions to ask, and the right people to ask them of, and I said: "Sure, I can handle that!" And you can too. All you need is a library and a telephone.

If you're in a small town, however, you may have to stay away from certain kinds of complicated assignments. Your library resources may be limited, and you won't be able to just pick up a phone to call people you may want to interview. In a big city you'll find the head offices of many corporations, universities, laboratories, teaching hospitals and so on. The cost would be prohibitive if you tried calling these places long distance from a small town. (Only a few large magazines will spring for unlimited phone calls.)

I'm not saying that you can't make a good living if you're miles away from where the action is—you can do anything you set your mind to. You'll probably just have to choose the ideas that you send to editors more carefully, and there will be much more paperwork all around. If I need to talk with a Vice President of the Sony Corporation, for example, I can just pick up my phone because he's right here. But if you're in Kansas somewhere, you'd probably have to write to him and then wait for a reply.

Of course there can be problems wherever you live. You have to learn exactly what resources are locally available to you. Spend a couple of days going all through your library. If there's a college or university within an easy distance there will be a lot more material in the library there, not to mention professors of all kinds to interview. But be realistic and know your limitations. If you're not in a town containing a lot of manufacturing plants, you wouldn't want to land an assignment that would require you to tour sixteen major plants and compare safety inspection procedures. Likewise if you live in the heart of New York City and do not drive, you might not be able to do an assignment that would require you to interview three dozen farm families. (Sure, you could do it on the phone, but your long distance bill would be more than the fee you'd get for the article.)

There are of course other limitations that have nothing to do with where you live. If you're strongly anti-abortion or anti-Democrat, a zealous athiest or Zionist, if you hate dogs or think that the money spent saving the whales could be much better spent feeding homeless pigeons, or whatever, these things may prevent you from doing an unbiased article on certain subjects.

The point of this is simple. You don't want to have to turn down an impossible or difficult assignment **after** it's been offered to you, because that reflects badly on your professionalism. So you have to know and understand your limitations—whatever they are—before you send in ideas for consideration. (In other words, if you hate opera, don't suggest articles that would require you to go to the opera!) There are five zillion other things to write about.

A big part of succeeding as a freelancer is flexibility. Within the limitations of your circumstances, of course, you have to be willing to do a lot of different things. If you're only willing to write about things you already know, and don't like doing research and interviews, you will have trouble finding work. Research and interviewing come with the job, and are a necessary and important part of it.

Let's say you suggest an idea to an editor, and he likes it. He calls you up and tells you that you can have the assignment, but only if you'll interview 36 nuclear physicists about the premise. You are certainly free to tell the editor that you're not willing to do that many interviews—but you may never get offered another assignment from him unless you can convince him that the article would be just as good if you interview only five or seven physicists. You have to remember that there are always writers around who would be perfectly willing to interview 36 people for an article, and editors want to work with willing writers.

If you want to become a full-time writer, you will just have to be able to handle almost anything. You may start out specializing in house plants, which is great and will get you into a few publications quickly and easily, but there is a finite number of markets for your house plant articles. Sooner or later you will have to branch out if you want to keep busy and/or make a decent living.

I have had months when I have had to write eighteen different articles on eighteen different subjects entirely. (Did I hear you gasp? If you really want to write full-time and make a full-time income, you'll be doing that too eventually. Articles generally don't pay enough to enable us to only write a couple a month.)

So the answer to "What Should You Write?" should be simply WHATEVER THE EDITORS WANT. If you want to be successful, you'll have to learn to be resourceful and adaptable—so start out confidently that way.

It will take you longer to research and write an article about a subject you know nothing about—but it can be done. If you're too picky about the assignments you will accept, you may find that nobody wants you.

When you're well-established and/or famous, then you can pick and choose among assignments—but not when you're starting out. If you can prove to the editors that you can indeed handle almost anything—no matter how dumb or obscure—you'll find them giving you better and better things to work on.

WHAT NOW?

You need three things if you want to make it as a writer. And there's no way around any of them—you do need them all. But the good news is that if you're lacking in any, you can always learn!

First, you have to be able to write reasonably well. Second, you have to know how to market what you produce. And third, you have to have some self-confidence, some courage, to go after what you want. (Nobody is going to hand you anything on a silver platter.)

Let's explore each of these things in turn.

You must be able to write reasonably well. Not spectacularly, just reasonably well. You have to be able to take your subject and tell people about it in print. You need to put appropriate words and phrases together smoothly and correctly so that what you produce sounds good to the ear. (An excellent way to check on this is simply to have someone read something you've written back to you out loud. If it sounds odd or stilted, your writing needs some polish.)

Editors do not expect perfection. And they also do not want formal, stilted prose containing so many fancy words that it sounds like you write with a dictionary in one hand. Now some magazines expect a tighter style than others, and some do want a lot of big words—but a loose, easy style, like I'm using to write this book, has never done me wrong. Most magazines want writing that sounds like you're talking with a good friend. And some editors have told me that it is this easy style of mine which has assured my success.

Of course, some magazines do want fancy writing with big words. And that is why you have to study the magazines you would like to write for. (See the chapters on query writing.) But you probably don't need to worry about this sort of magazine at the beginning of your career. "Heavy" magazines—The Economist is one of many good examples —are not interested in beginners anyway. You have to have established a solid reputation in both your field and in the field of writing before you could land an assignment from a magazine like that.

Generally, remember that you have to write for two people. You have to of course please the editor of the magazine—but you also must keep the magazine's audience in mind as you write. If, for example, you're writing an article on new strides in preventing eye diseases in cats for a Veterinary journal, you'll certainly use technical terms and very detailed descriptions. If you're doing the same story for a general-circulation magazine about pets, you'll have to take a different approach entirely. If you turned in the first article to the pet magazine, or the latter article to the journal, you'd be rejected on the spot.

The point of this is that you can't always write the way you want to. You have your own "style" of writing—we all do. And your style may be fabulous. But you will not always be able to write in your own style. If you want to sell your work—and that means both pleasing the editor and appealing to a given magazine's readers—you'll have to be willing to adapt to the magazine's basic style.

But take heart. Even though you might feel that you can write only one way, that is not true. Give yourself a chance—you'll find that you're much more flexible than you think.

I believe that writers are **made,** not born. Granted, some people seem to take naturally to a pen and never need any formal training. But I feel that anyone who really **wants** to write better **can.** There are some excellent books out about how to write, many school classes, correspondence courses, adult education classes, etc. If you are serious about making it as a writer, your first step is to learn to write reasonably well.

You probably have a stack of things that you've already written. Take a couple of your best and ask a local high school or college English teacher to read them over and give you an honest evaluation. (If it's somebody who doesn't know you, all the better—sorry, but you just cannot trust your friends and loved ones!) Or take your stuff to two or three teachers for an even better evaluation. Ask them to review the articles or stories for construction, grammar, punctuation, etc., and not for content, subject matter or depth of research.

You can also hire a professional editor to do this job, but be careful which one you choose. Some "editorial services" or "evaluation services" that advertise in writers' magazines, supermarket tabloids and other places are not seriously interested in helping you. All they want is for you to become a client. They will tell you whatever they need to tell you so that you might sign on with their editing service or take one of their writing courses.

If you'd like to get some serious help from a real editor, your best bet is to look up some kind of freelance editors association or writers association in your area. Call them and ask for a referral. Most of these associations have certain members who enjoy helping new writers, and you may even find someone to really take you under his or her wing. The one-to-one help and advice you can get from someone like this will be incomparable.

The freelance editors association I belong to, for example, has set up a "manuscript evaluation" service which certain members take part in—and I for one just LOVE doing it. We'll read up to four chapters (depending on length) of any book, or four articles, and give the author a very detailed several-page evaluation covering everything from what (if anything) the writing style needs, to the prospects of getting the book or articles published and a list of possible publishers, for only $100. (See page 143 for more information.)

Once you know what you are doing wrong (if anything) or how you might make some improvements, you can work on making your writing better. Think of the time you spend getting better as an investment in your future. You may think that a class would be expensive—but have you ever tried adding up all the money you've spent on paper, envelopes, photocopies and stamps, sending out bad or inadequate manuscripts only to have them returned?

Remember that you would need training for whatever kind of job you'd want to land—sometimes for years and years. Learning to write reasonably well is not hard—it just takes the desire on your part. If you go after it with everything you've got, it won't take very long at all.

If you feel that there is something lacking in your writing, and you are seriously not willing to learn to write better, there is also a way around that. You can always hire someone from a writers or editors association to fix up your stuff before you hand it in. This will get expensive, but if you really want to get published, this can be done. However, be warned that it will be almost impossible to keep this up for long. You'll be found out sooner or later.

Marketing what you produce is as important as the writing. If you spend all of your time locked away in an attic writing, you may have absolutely wonderful stuff—but nobody will ever know about it.

Chances are, however, that you've been sending manuscripts out—and probably getting most or all of them returned. But like the girl I spoke with at that party, you may simply be setting your sights a little too high at this point of your career.

But while fancy glossy national magazines may not seem to have the time of day for you, there **are** magazines in desperate need of writers. And there is no reason why you cannot be one of them!

I'm talking of course about new and/or small magazines. Some of these magazines actually fold, go bankrupt, because they cannot find any good writers to fill the pages. Advertisers don't continue to advertise in magazines that print garbage or just plain stupid articles.

It may sound incredible to you that some magazines can't find writers when there are five zillion writers out there anxious to be published— but it is really, unfortunately true that most of these writers just never hook up with somebody who really needs them.

Now you may have been ignoring these small or new magazines because you simply never thought about contacting them, or perhaps you thought the pay was too low. Everybody thinks first about the biggies— and that is precisely why there's so much competition there, and why your chances of getting published there as a newcomer are slight. But as you read this book there are thousands of perfectly good magazines that would absolutely love to meet a couple of good reliable freelancers. Yes, like you!

Granted, the pay may be low at many of them. (And at some of them the pay is surprisingly not low.) But if you can get in solid with a magazine and can write three, four—maybe even more—articles per issue, all those little fees add up quite nicely. That singles tabloid I wrote for in 1979-80 only paid seven cents a word—but I wrote thousands and thousands of words each week. I was able to support myself on seven cents a word.

Some people feel that writing for small magazines is "below them", or that their talent and ideas are too good to "waste" on small magazines. If this is the way you think, you may never get published unless you change some of your ideas. There is absolutely nothing wrong with "paying your dues" or "starting out in the mail room". Most people in most fields of endeavor start out at the bottom and work their way up.

Depending on how fast you can work, how much you can produce, this may take many months—or even years—but it's a steady upward climb. And you cannot help but succeed if you follow all the guidelines given in this book.

Of course you may find that you enjoy the people at some of these small magazines so much that you'll never want to "move up" to bigger markets. Many people make perfectly good livings writing for little magazines. You have to write more stuff, but each article is shorter and requires less work than, say, something for Reader's Digest, which can take months to research and write.

With small magazines you also have one perk that you don't usually have at big national magazines, and you may find that this is very important to you. (It was to me when I started out.) You have more freedom to write what you want at a new or small magazine. If you write a cooking article for some really big national magazine, let's say, they probably tell you what they want you to write and how to write it. It has to tie in with the rest of the magazine. But at a little magazine chances are good that you can decide what to do and how you'll do it.

Small magazines also do not usually do as much editing as large ones do. Of course the editor will still fix your article up if it has any deficiencies, but he probably won't totally rewrite it the way some national magazines do. There are some magazines that you can actually identify just by looking at something they've printed—because every article sounds the same. They're all rewritten to the same exact style and tone. I'm not saying that's bad—they know what sells their magazines, and they didn't get to be big national magazines by alienating their audience. But if you're someone who has a style all your own, and would really like to see it in print just that way, you'll probably be treated much better at a smaller magazine.

Finding these special magazines is not hard at all. Many of them are listed in the *Writer's Market* and *The Writer's Handbook*. Even more appear in a yearly book called *The International Directory of Little Magazines and Small Presses*. But do keep in mind that any magazine that has a listing anywhere is probably not in dire need of writers because there are thousands of new writers searching these directories for markets.

The best way to find small and new magazines is to simply go to the biggest magazine store in your town and have a really thorough look at what's there. Most of the tips explained in a later chapter of this book, How To Find New Magazines, work equally well for finding small magazines.

Follow the exact same method you'd use if you were contacting the top magazine in the country—and that includes using professional printed stationery, dressing up when you visit the editor, etc. He will be so impressed with your professionalism that you'll probably get a lot of work from him.

For many small magazines don't always attract a high percentage of really professional people.

The day you walk into his life will probably be the beginning of a long and happy relationship for both of you!

This, of course, brings us to the last necessary quality, **self-confidence or courage.** I'll be the first to admit that it takes a lot of guts to write to someone who has never heard of you and to tell him that you're anxious to get some work from him. It takes even more guts to follow through on some of the methods given in a later chapter for finding new magazines.

But if you really want to make it as a writer you have to go after what you want. You cannot, unfortunately, sit at home and write all the time, figuring that "talent will out" and that someone will come to you. It doesn't work that way.

You have to develop your writing as well as you can and then go confidently out into the world and convince other people that you're good. The first few times will be terrifying, but it does get easier, I promise.

Now editors deal with a lot of writers, and they know that many of us are shy, quiet or temperamental. Sometimes these qualities actually go with the territory—they're actually a part of what makes us creative. (This is why many writers hire an agent as soon as they can, so that they don't have to deal with anything personally.)

But you have to do your best to overcome any problems you might have in this area when you're starting out in your writing career. If you're too scared or shy to go after what you want, it's obvious that you'll never get it. Writers who are confident of their skills get the most work because they plunge right in and ask for it. In other words, if you're always **there,** how can the editor keep refusing you?

Of course you don't want to appear too egotistical—this has killed the budding careers of an awful lot of writers. No editor wants to work with someone who thinks he's God's gift. But you have to be confident of your ability to handle an assignment, any assignment, and to tell the editor so. If you have any problems with self-confidence, it might be worth your time and money to take a class in motivation, developing your potential, etc. There are also many good books on this subject. (Start with *Feel Free* by David Viscott.)

Once you have mastered these three points, nothing will stop you!

THE QUERY LETTER

When I started writing, I didn't know what I was doing. Sad but true—I wasted many years. I started out unfortunately like most people do even today—hit and miss. (And almost always miss.)

I wrote hundreds of short stories and poems while I was in high school and university. I'd do them as best I could, then wrap them up and ship them off somewhere. I had never heard of the *Writer's Market* or *The Writer's Handbook.* I lived in a small town, which didn't even have a big book and magazine store, and our local racks didn't carry either The Writer or Writer's Digest. I knew almost nothing. All I knew is that I wanted to write.

So I wrote stuff. I sent manuscripts to the magazines I knew and read—Seventeen, Glamour, Teen, etc.

And every single one of them came back. I never to this day have had a piece of fiction or a poem published (other than in high school and university literary magazines, which I feel don't "count"). And I didn't get a piece of non-fiction published until I did something for free when I was 24. I could have given up, of course, but I'm stubborn, and I didn't. It took me literally **years** to learn how to get something published.

These days there are a lot of good books about writing and getting published. But I guess that most people either don't read them, or else don't believe what they say—because every day I see people doing the same things I did when I was starting out. The same **wrong** things. But since this book contains no bull, as promised, you can believe everything that's written here. It took me a long time to figure out the system, but now I know the way things really work. If you are serious about making it as a writer, you have a few things to learn too.

You will probably never get anything published by just writing things and sending them out. It didn't happen 20 years ago, and it won't happen now when there is much more competition. Of course it does happen occasionally, but it's hardly worth depending on. Competition is very keen. There are so many people who want to be writers these days. So many manuscripts are sent in unsolicited. And many editors are so busy that much (or all) of the unsolicited material is never even looked at. (That doesn't just apply to fiction—many non-fiction magazines return manuscripts unopened or unread too. Or it may have been opened and returned in your SASE with a printed note or rejection slip attached—but that does not mean that it was really read.)

Yes, of course, many editors eagerly look through the slush piles seeking new undiscovered gems of talent. And yes, some people **have** gotten started that way. But geesh, chances of this happening are small. Going the unsolicited manuscript route is truly the **hard way** of going about getting published. It is also the most expensive way—in time and in money.

To send out an unsolicited manuscript you have to write it first. That time will have been wasted if nobody wants your idea or article. (Although do understand that writing time is never really wasted—every article or story you do is helping you gain experience and become a better writer. But if your main goal is to get published and to make money, writing things you don't have contracts for is a waste of your time—valuable time that could be much better spent looking for paying assignments.)

You also can waste a lot of money sending out unsolicited manuscripts—money spent on photocopies, envelopes, stamps, etc.

However, if you approach getting published the right way, it's a million times easier. So what is the right way?

It's called the query letter. If you've read anything at all about writing, you'll know about query letters. But chances are good that if you're unpublished, you either haven't tried them, or else haven't given them a good and fair chance. They're the only way to go!

Editors are unbelievably busy. When it's December, they're probably sweating about articles that are late for the February issue, trying to edit articles for the March issue, and trying to select ideas and make assignments for April and May and maybe June, all at the same time. Especially at medium-to-large magazines, the editors almost never have time to even open their own mail, and certainly never have time to read some article sent in unsolicited from someone they've never even heard of. Believe that.

But they love to read **letters** from writers! Their secretaries will probably set these aside in a special place because they're so very important. Remember that the main job of an editor is to put out a good magazine. If he doesn't do this, consistently, he's out. His job is on the line every single month, with every single issue. (And if he's also the owner of the magazine, he's even more worried, because he has to have a good magazine so that people will buy it and his wife and kids in the suburbs will have food on the table next month.) And all of this stuff can make a man nervous.

An editor is always looking for superstar ideas, because it is ideas that make his magazine. He needs good, solid, timely, fabulous articles— lots of them, all the time. But he doesn't need only ideas—he also needs people to write them up into great articles. Most editors have a small stable of writers that they depend on month after month, simply because they have proven themselves—they've always been there for him. Always good new fresh ideas, and equally satisfactory articles.

Because you must have ideas, or the editor doesn't want you at all— even if you're the best writer in the city. You cannot just offer to write for a magazine—you must come up with ideas and tell the editor what you want to write. He is far too busy to think up twenty or more article ideas to fill each issue. So every day he scans—in just a few seconds— each query letter that crosses his threshold with ideas. He needs wonderful new ideas desperately.

So you have an excellent chance of reaching the editor with your ideas. But you only have a few seconds. He's probably only going to skim that letter of yours unless something really catches his eye. So you have to be sure that something does!

Once you have made the decision to start pursuing your writing career in the most professional manner, your first step is deciding which magazine you would like to write for first (or next). If you already have a great idea, go to your city's biggest magazine store and look at all of the magazines that seem appropriate for that idea, and buy copies or jot down the names so that you can read them in the library.

Another alternative is to spend an hour or so with a copy of the *Writer's Market* or *The Writer's Handbook,* looking for magazines that would be interested in the article you'd like to do, and then buy copies or read them in the library. If you cannot find some magazines that are listed, you'll have to send away for sample issues—and this takes time.

If you have your heart set on getting a specific article in one specific magazine, you're best off to wait until you've sent away for the writer's guidelines before you submit your query. (Be sure to follow the rules listed in the *Writer's Market* or *The Writer's Handbook* concerning getting each magazine's guidelines. Most will want at least an SASE, and in some cases this request goes to a specific person or even a different address.) It's worth the time. Your query will be much better received if you follow the advice given in the guidelines.

Most guidelines are pretty much the same, but occasionally there are some that are really unique. If a given magazine wants something really different from the writers, it will be good to know this ahead of time. Do not just rely on the market listings for information on what a magazine specifically wants. Although I do not know personally of any magazines that have a "blacklist" or any such thing, I do know from personal experience as an editor that some totally inappropriate or dumb query letters do stick in the mind, along with the name of their authors. It's best not to take any chances. You wouldn't want to make an irreparable mistake in the beginning of your career that may close the door to some magazine forever.

The worst query I've ever received? It was a poor photocopy of an original, and started with the words: "To Whom It May Concern:"—needless to say I remember who wrote it. (I replied by sending her a copy of the promotional flyer for this book, but she never ordered one.) It's for reasons like this that some people never get published.

Once you've decided on which magazine you want to approach, your next step is research—you must do your homework. This is vital, and cannot be overlooked. Go to a library and really look at the last twelve issues of the magazine you'd like to work for. (Now that you're taking your writing seriously, you'll want to buy or subscribe to and save all issues of all the magazines you plan on writing for. This will make it easy to look up things in the future.) As you look through every page, make notes on which topics have been covered, which are constantly covered, approximate length of articles, and type—narrative, first person, third person, etc. This will take a little time, but is imperative. If you were to suggest an article to an editor that his magazine just carried three issues ago, he will think that you don't know what's going on. Even worse yet, he will know that you don't read his precious, wonderful magazine!

If you want to be totally safe, you might even check the last few issues of the magazine's closest competitors. If you ever visit the offices of a large magazine, you'll see that they have a wall somewhere, filled with shelves or little cubicles. If you look closely, you'll note that these cubicles contain all the back issues (for at least a year) of all the magazines that even vaguely compete with it. So don't ever think that you can "borrow" ideas from other magazines, and that the editor won't know. He follows his competition very closely, and keeps the old issues at hand so that he can always check something.

However, you will find that you're getting dozens of wonderful ideas just by looking through old issues of the magazines you want to write for (and others). Almost everything you see will trigger something else in your mind, if you've trained yourself to be alert for possible article subjects. Jot down every idea that flashes into your mind, and you can develop them later. When you've come up with three or four good solid ideas that are in the style of the magazine you want to write for, but not things that have just been done, you're ready to write your query.

By the way, beware of coming up with ideas that are too far removed from the sort of thing the magazine has been publishing. You might think: "This guy has never ever done anything that even mentions space exploration, so he must be dying to have a story like that. I'll send him this great space shuttle idea".

In actuality, if he's never done anything even remotely about space exploration, chances are good that he doesn't **want** anything about space exploration. Stick with ideas that are similar in tone and vein to those already printed—you'll have a much better chance. The last thing you want is for him to think: "She must not even read the magazine—she doesn't have a **clue** about the kind of things we publish!"

Select your best three or four ideas, based on the homework you've done with the old issues, the competition's old issues, and the market listings, which tell you outright what the editor's looking for (if his magazine is listed). All three of these sources are important—don't overlook any of them. It's really important that you gather a "feel" for magazines before you query them, so that the editors will be impressed with your grasp of their magazines' content and purpose. (And that could never hurt.)

When you read the most current issue of the magazine, also make note of the correct spelling of the current correct editor's name. The market book you have may be more than a year old, and editors tend to move around a lot—so never send a query without checking the most recent masthead.

If the magazine you're interested in is in a market book, or if you have a set of writer's guidelines, one or both should tell you to whom your query should be addressed. If there is only one editor, of course he gets it. But it can get tricky if there are a dozen editors and the market books or guidelines don't offer any help.

This is a general guide: Never send anything to the publisher, and never send anything to an "executive editor" unless the guidelines or market book tell you differently. You can send your queries to almost anyone else. Editors are listed on the masthead in order of rank, so if it feels right, send to the first name on the masthead (after the executive editor, if there is one). But this top guy will be the busiest person at the magazine, and it will probably take longer to hear something back on your query.

I generally query one of the "senior editors", or whatever title is given to the person or persons a notch or two below the big guy. I choose one whose name I like. And if I don't like the response I get, I might try someone else the next time. All of the lower-ranked editors are expected to come up with great ideas too—any magazine big enough to have a whole bunch of editors usually has story meetings where ideas are discussed, and each editor is expected to contribute something.

A lower-ranked editor who is ambitious will definitely be looking to discover some good writers and fabulous ideas. He or she will generally be a little less busy than the main editor, and will probably have a little extra time for you too—perhaps to work with you and to help you develop appropriate ideas (which will eventually enhance his or her advancement).

Whichever editor you choose, be absolutely positive that you have spelled the name correctly. Editors—especially those with strange names— are always getting sloppy queries with their names spelled wrong. And I guarantee you that they will be hesitant to trust you with an assignment if you can't handle something as simple as looking up and copying a name correctly.

The query itself should be no more than two pages single spaced. One page is fine, but I've always figured that as long as I'm writing I might as well send at least 3-4 ideas (unless the magazine was listed in a market book and the listing warned to only send one idea at a time, or this information was given in the writer's guidelines). But don't worry if you have only one great idea—the editor will be glad to get it.

You'll want to work up a couple of paragraphs on each idea—not pages and pages. More important than even the idea itself is telling the editor which **approach** you want to take with the idea.

On any particular Monday morning he may get twenty-nine letters all stating: "I'd love to do an article on the space shuttle!", and only one that states: "I'd like to do an article on the ways the space shuttle may be used twenty years from now—travelling routinely to the moon, hauling garbage into space for disposal, visiting the space stations, etc."

In other words, your letter is worthless to the editor unless you go into some detail about your approach, what you'd like to do with your idea. (Ideas are literally a dime a dozen.) He doesn't have time to enter into a lengthy correspondence with you (or even to give you a call if you're in town) to ascertain exactly what you have in mind.

You may not realize it, but editors of national magazines get hundreds of letters every week. And as much as you may think that your article idea is unique, it probably isn't. You get your ideas the same way every writer does. You see things, you hear things. Perhaps the title of a TV special triggers something and gives you a great idea. Well, the same idea is undoubtedly occurring to thousands of other writers at the same moment. We all have a collective memory and history, you know. If the idea you come up with is really fabulous, don't wait to send it off. If it's just what the editor has been waiting for, it may be a case of first-come, first-assigned.

So some weeks it's not unlikely that any given editor will receive 50 queries about the exact same thing. A truly unique idea is very rare. But a unique approach—now that's something else! It's the writer with the truly unique approach that will get the assignment.

Of course it goes without saying that you have to tell the editor what you have in mind. Your plan for developing the idea may indeed be the very best one, but he will never know unless you tell him. He can't read your mind through a letter. It really is a waste of time—both for the editor and for yourself—if you just send out letters on the order of: "I have always wanted to do an article on the space shuttle, and know a lot about it. What would you like?"

Even worse is something like this: "I really want to write for your magazine, and I like writing about space exploration, dogs and African flowers. Can I do something for you?"

These letters are totally worthless, and may even get pitched by the secretary before hitting the editor's desk. Remember, he's got too much to do already without reading worthless pieces of correspondence—and that's exactly what these two examples are.

If you have been sending out queries like this—congratulations for at least sending out queries instead of unsolicited manuscripts—but please stop immediately. If you've gotten replies to letters like this you've been very lucky, or were dealing with small magazines that were in such desperate need of writers that they'd go after anybody or anything.

The secret to succeeding in the world of professional writing is just that—looking at all times like a professional writer. And professional writers, and even writers with a couple of dozen things in print, know that they have to send good, detailed queries. Any letter like the above examples brands you loudly and clearly as an amateur—and many editors avoid amateurs like the plague.

Remember that, unless you're very famous already, editors don't want YOU, per se. They want what you can **do,** your ideas. You may be the best writer in the world, but unless you can come up with some good ideas, most magazines won't be interested in you. After all, anybody can write to an editor and state that he's a great writer, just waiting for an assignment and instructions. (And believe me, many people do!) As I mentioned before, the editor is much too busy to think up the dozens of ideas for articles his magazine needs each and every month. (And he knows that even if he did, the magazine would probably be boring and wouldn't last long.) He really needs fabulous creative input from dozens or hundreds of good writers all over the place, all coming up with variations on solid ideas. If you can give him this regularly, believe me, your letters will be anticipated with the proverbial baited breath.

Of utmost importance is your letter. You should have professional printed stationery. And your letter must be typewritten. If you don't take care of these two things, you'll really look like an amateur—just what the editor doesn't want or need. You have to type, and type well. If you can't do a good job, have someone type the query for you. If your letter hits the editor's desk with a dozen spelling or typing mistakes, lots of correction fluid or strikeovers, he will immediately see that you're sloppy—and probably would never trust you with an assignment. Your letter must be **perfect.**

A very big part of writing professionally is **being serious about your work.** And if your letter—your first introduction to an editor—looks bad, you don't have to guess what he is going to think of you. (They say that you only have one chance to make a good first impression.)

You don't have to have expensive embossed stationery—but do have something (and be sure that it has your phone number). Printed stationery is much more important than a business card, which most writers do have—so if you cannot afford both, at least get the stationery. But you'll find that if you have both, and they match, this looks good.

Typing with a crisp black ribbon is also essential. If the letter looks good, the editor will be much more receptive to your ideas. If you seriously can't type, or if all you have is an old Underwood that doesn't even type a straight line anymore, you can easily find somebody to do up your letters. Most colleges have students willing to take on small typing jobs for a reasonable fee, or you can probably find somebody in your local newspaper under "Temporary Help Wanted" or "Secretarial Services". (If your typing is that bad you'll also need someone to type up your manuscripts, so it's good to find somebody reliable right from the beginning.)

It is imperative to remember that your query letter is also a sample of your writing. If it sounds too stilted, too casual, or is full of grammatical or spelling errors, the editor will (and probably correctly) assume that that is the way you write articles too. If you're not sure of the way your letter looks or sounds, have somebody read it over before you send it out.

Although style is important, I don't agree with some authors of books on writing who tell you that your queries should always be snappy and funny. I've found that a straightforward, honest approach is best. Of course, there are ideas appropriate for snappy and funny, but serious topics demand serious queries.

Your best bet may be something unusual—but not too unusual!—to catch the editor's eye. I would guess that 90% of the queries any editor gets are pretty much the same, in look and substance, so something that stands out just a little should be impressive as long as it doesn't go overboard. (I have found that a very well-designed and distinctive letterhead gets attention. I've even had editors scribble notes to me on the bottom of letters about how much they like my letterhead.)

Be very careful that you don't use any phrases like: "You should run this article!", or "This is the best idea you'll ever see!", or "I'm the only one who can do this the right way!" Or any other such things. You do want to present yourself as capable and confident, but don't get carried away. If you say things like this, the editor may think you'll be impossible to work with because of your ego problems!

Speak openly and honestly. I usually tell the editor that I've read and enjoyed the magazine for a long time, and that I really would like to write something for him. And that I've come up with some ideas I think he will like. I present the ideas clearly and simply, using a quote or anecdote only if appropriate. I frequently go into a semi-outline form, using arrows or asterisks to mark the different points, when I feel that this is the best way to cover an approach that has several facets.

If the ideas are short and sweet, then just make them so with one paragraph each. If you ramble, trying to fill space, the editor will probably assume your articles will be like that too.

Once you have successfully worked with an editor a few times, and he or she knows your style, you may just be able to submit lists of ideas with only a sentence or two about each idea. I got a great assignment once with only these few words: "A day in the life of a rape crisis center". It was all that needed to be said.

There are many writers who feel that they must do a lot of research before sending out a query, and that every query must truly be a miniature of the whole, with a beginning, middle and ending. There will indeed be some complicated topics that will require some semblance of this approach, but generally I feel that this is a waste of time and energy. You should do just enough research to find out if there is really a story to be told, and if your approach or premise is logical (and if the article can be written the way you'd like to do it). For example, you may be anxious to do an article for your local paper to expose some state senators you feel or heard are taking bribes. This would indeed be a great story—if somebody is taking bribes. You would have to have some concrete facts before you could think about doing an article like that. This is an example of an instance where heavy research is absolutely vital before submitting the query.

But take your space shuttle idea. It should not be at all hard to find a dozen scientists or astronomers who would have an interesting opinion about how the space shuttle will be used twenty years from now. If you have easy access to one, you might want to ask him about it and then (briefly) mention his theory as an example of the type of opinion you hope to get from all of the people you plan to interview—but I certainly would not make any long distance calls to Carl Sagan asking for an opinion— and therefore wasting his very valuable time—just to write a query! Remember that no matter how fabulous you think an idea is, you may never ever be able to sell it. Nobody may ever want it. (This has happened to me more times than I care to say.) So be careful about wasting too much of your own and other people's time before you actually have an assignment.

Be careful, too, when writing a query about something you're passionately interested or involved in. Try not to get carried away. Too much detail on any given query may serve to turn the editor off—he doesn't need to know all kinds of minutiae to know if he wants the article or not. (And you wouldn't want him to think that your articles are full of useless minutiae either, would you? He'd hate that, because it would mean extra time editing!)

Try to give only as much information as necessary, so that the editor can clearly see exactly where you want to go with the topic, and so that he can see that you know what you're talking about—and no more, and no less.

I usually close my queries with something like this: "I hope that you like these ideas, but if they're not appropriate at this time, I'll be glad to send in some more. I'd really like to become a regular contributor to your magazine—I hope you'll give me an opportunity to show you what I can do." I thank him for his time, and say that I hope I'll hear from him soon.

Don't mention that you've enclosed a self-addressed stamped envelope; it is assumed that you've done this. Remember—you have to come across like an old pro—not like this is the first editor you've ever written to (even if he is).

So it goes without saying that you should never tell an editor if you haven't been published. If you've had a couple of things in print, and if they're good enough, have crisp plain-paper photocopies made of them, and tell him that you're enclosing "a couple assorted samples of my work".

If you're totally unpublished, or have only had less-than-great things published, just don't say anything. Your letter should be good enough to stand on its own. (And if it's not, you shouldn't send it out.) If you've had some little things published in community newspapers or high school bulletins, don't send these along unless they're outstanding features. Almost anybody can get published in those places, and if the editor thinks this is all you have it may lower his opinion of you. Remember—the key to getting an assignment is looking like a professional, not an amateur.

When I was an editor some people sent me unpublished, completed manuscripts as samples of their work. I know that I didn't care to read them, as they were usually on boring topics—that's probably why they were unpublished—and I put much more stock in the query letter itself. I would think that sending manuscripts like this would work against you, even if they are really good. The editor would probably either consider them unsolicited submissions, even if you told him they were just samples, or would wonder why you haven't sent him something that's been published. Unpublished manuscripts are just that—orphans that nobody wanted.

And for that same reason I would never tell an editor that I had dozens of articles all ready to send to him to look at (all that stuff you've been writing for the past few years and couldn't get published or haven't even tried to sell). He might wonder if they had all been written on assignment for some other magazine, and then rejected—or worse. What's worse? That you just sit home and write all the time and are never able to sell anything.

If you do have a great article available for some reason—perhaps it was rejected by some other magazine (when this happens it is not always your fault) or perhaps you just got incredibly inspired some night and wrote your little heart out—don't ever tell an editor that. Pretend like it hasn't been written yet, and query him just like you're starting from scratch. If he buys the approach to the idea as it was written, you will have saved yourself a lot of work and can impress him by turning it in early. Even if it needs minor (or even major) adjustments, you can still turn it in early.

In addition to your perfect letter, what else should you send to the editor? Many writers have a resume, and this is not a bad idea if you've had a few things published or if you have some impressive job experience that you feel may help you get assignments in a given area. I didn't make one up until I had been published in eight different magazines, figuring it would have worked against me if I had only one or two to list.

My resume now consists of two pages, one of which lists all of the magazines I've been published in and what I did for them—feature articles, cooking column, book reviews, etc. The first page of the resume lists my education, writing awards I have won, professional writing and editing associations I belong to, and all the areas I specialize in or have better-than-average knowledge of. I also have a paragraph on how well I've done with my writing, a paragraph on my editing experience, and a paragraph on the books I have written and the ones I'm working on.

If you have some particular experience that would sound impressive—perhaps if you've been CEO of some company, or had your own business—I think you should add this. Do not, however, submit to an editor a standard business-type resume, listing every little job you've had and the dates, and every little thing you do in your spare time, like hobbies, volunteer work, etc. Use only things that are relevant to the job at hand—writing. (Of course, some volunteer work may be appropriate—perhaps you edited your company's newsletter, or wrote brochures or ad copy for a hospital, etc.)

If you feel that you don't have enough information to make up a resume, that's perfectly okay—don't worry about it. Anything that can be said in a resume can be said in your letter—and should be said if you have any special experience or knowledge of the subject you're querying about.

This helps an editor get to know you, and this is never a bad idea. Each day he gets all of these letters from all kinds of people he doesn't know. Anything that you can do (within reason) to make yourself stand out as a special individual is always helpful.

If, for example, you're querying about an article on some medical topic, by all means mention if you've had a year of medical school or some nurse's training. If you're just a very educated layman, you can say that too. If you don't blow your own horn a little, the editor will never know that you're special.

You'll also need to enclose a few tearsheets with your query if you have some good ones. Four or five is an ideal number, and if you have a lot of different ones to choose from, try to send those which are relevant to the topic. Send some health article tearsheets when querying about a health article, etc.

If you don't have many samples to choose from, it's okay just to send one. Just be sure that it's good. If you really don't have anything good, it's okay not to send anything. The editor may call or write and ask for some samples of your work, and in that case, you'll have to fess up. But if your letter is perfect and full of wonderful, appropriate ideas, he may just assume that you know what you're doing and not need to see any samples.

As you get more and more things published, keep upgrading the quality of your samples. Any tearsheets you send should be good enough to stand on their own, and you shouldn't have to make excuses for them. My first few really good articles were plagued with typesetting errors, and I was almost ashamed to send them out. But they were my best articles. In a case like this, don't worry—any editor who reads them will know that things like this are not the writer's fault.

If there are errors in facts or figures, however, or other kinds of blatant mistakes, the editor knows that these are probably the writer's fault. Do not send something like this as a sample, and then spend half a page of your letter explaining why you made the mistakes or how it wasn't really your fault. If you feel some excuses or explanations are necessary, don't send that particular article to an editor when looking for work—it will only work against you.

And I can't say this often enough—find yourself a good printer with really good equipment. So many photocopies I see are horrible—light in color, blurry, and with all kinds of debris on the paper. It really is important to present a totally professional image, and copies like this are just garbage. A good printer will keep trying various settings on his best equipment until he can make you wonderful crisp photocopies—keep looking until you find such a fantastic guy. It costs no more to have a good copy made.

Now I realize that magazines print articles in all sorts of different (and sometimes absolutely ludicrous) ways, sometimes even with continuations of single paragraphs on each of dozens of different pages. Take a copy or two of the magazine and carefully cut out all the little pieces of your article and fit them together in the proper sequence and glue them onto a master page or two to use for your photocopying. Make sure that everything you send out is on a standard 8½" x 11" piece of paper. (Occasionally a legal size paper is okay—but with the proper equipment, almost any size original can be fitted onto a standard size piece of paper for duplication. Ask your printer.) There is nothing I hated more when I was an editor than to open an envelope and have dozens of little pieces of paper, all different sizes, fall out onto my desk. Even if they were clipped together, those little pieces are a pain to try to read. Glue all of your little pieces onto standard pieces of paper, and have them photocopied that way.

Many writers just write brief letters to editors covering only their article ideas and nothing else. Usually they will state something like: "Samples of my work available on request".

Now if you send a lot of queries around—and you'll have to if you want a reasonable amount of work—I realize that it can get expensive to send four or five samples to everybody. There's the extra postage as well as the bigger envelope and the photocopying costs. Many people feel that the chances of any given editor not wanting any given idea are great, and therefore you shouldn't waste extra time and money until you know if he likes the idea. There is some wisdom to this, so if you'd like to try sending only a one-page letter (and an SASE of course), you can certainly do this. I have never done it, so I do not know how you will be received. If the editor loves your idea, he will certainly not let the opportunity of hiring you pass, and will contact you for more details on yourself or your work if he wants them.

I have never done things this way because I always felt that it was too superficial. I have always subscribed to the theory of treating editors like they were very, very special—and I do as much as possible to make their job easier. (If they have to call or write you for samples or details on your experience in the area you want to write on, that is extra work for them.) But then again, when I was an editor it was true that at least 90% of the ideas I got were inappropriate, overdone, silly, or already assigned. So I certainly didn't mind not having all those pieces of paper to shuffle through when I knew in an instant that the ideas weren't wanted anyway.

On the other hand, I found a couple of articles among the samples that were sent me that I wanted to buy second rights to. And I have had the rare case when somebody called me and said that although they didn't like the original ideas I sent in, they did want to buy reprint rights to one of the samples I sent. So you can balance these points before you decide if it's right for you to send samples out or not.

I know of some writers who send every query by either registered mail or by courier. I feel that there are occasional cases when couriers are warranted, and I explain these in the chapter on finding new magazines. But it can get much too expensive to use these methods all the time. Remember, most of the ideas you send out will not get you assignments. You may feel that all of your ideas are uniquely fabulously special, but most of them will not be. You'll have to keep all kinds of queries circulating all the time to get a reasonable amount of work.

Always include a self-addressed stamped envelope. Always—if it's your first query to a magazine or your one-hundredth—unless the editor tells you specifically to stop sending them. Some rich magazines, like Reader's Digest, will tell you after a while to stop, but almost everybody else expects them. If you are sending things out without SASEs, you cannot complain if you do not get replies.

If you're sending a query to a magazine in another country, don't put your own postage on the SASE, because they will not be able to mail it. If possible, get a friend or relative to pick up some stamps during his next trip to that country, or some post offices will gladly send you stamps if you send them a money order. As a last resort only should you send those International Reply Coupons. They require a special trip to visit the post office clerk to use, and are not appreciated (and are frequently just tossed in the garbage).

Editors figure that if you really want to write for their magazines, you should be resourceful enough to get ahold of some postage stamps from their country.

Another note—please be sure that the envelope you send to the poor guy is big enough for the return of all of your stuff. Some very optimistic writers send only a little tiny envelope, hoping that all they'll get back is a little tiny letter of assignment or a little tiny contract. If you want your stuff back, be sure that the envelope is big enough and has enough postage on it.

Personally, I've found that once a resume and set of samples has passed twice through the mail system it is not in good enough shape to use again anyway. So I add, towards the end of my letter, "Please keep or toss the samples, as you wish, but I don't want them back". And I enclose a business-size SASE for only a letter of reply.

In this way the editor knows that you've sent him a fresh new set of samples, and that you probably wouldn't do that for 400 different editors. He will think that he's special, and what could that hurt?

This also allows the possibility that your samples will be saved in a file somewhere—and that you may get a call three years from now about an assignment. (Don't laugh—it happens.)

Above are the basics of the query letter—and they apply to large and small magazines alike. However, you will find that small and new magazines are much easier to approach than the biggies. They do not get the volume of mail that large national glossies and even medium-sized magazines do, and the editors are not quite as harried. Smaller magazines are also sometimes (although not always) in desperate need of good and dependable writers. Some of these magazines pay very little, by necessity, and they simply can't keep good writers. Many people just use them to get a little experience and then move on to bigger and better things.

But don't feel that you can take less care with a query to a small magazine. This editor has the same needs and problems, and actually probably sees a whole lot less professionalism all around. If your query is outstanding, he will be so happy that you want to write for his magazine that your chances of getting in are excellent—even if you've never been published before!

Most editors are educated and very smart people, and they can recognize quality when they see it. Make sure your queries are all quality—no matter where they're headed. They speak volumes about you!

MORE ON QUERIES

Once you've sent out your query the waiting begins. If you only have one query out in the world, it may seem like forever before it comes back. (A watched pot . . .) I recommend that you always have a lot of queries circulating. (If you haven't read my suggested method towards the end of the chapter entitled: Who Am I To Be Writing This Book?, you might want to now.) This is the only way you will really get a reasonable amount of work. If you wait until you've finished one assignment before you start looking for another, you'll be lucky to do three or four articles a year.

How long should you expect to wait? That depends on several things, the most important of which is probably how well-organized the magazine you're writing to is.

An editor who does his job in such a way that he never leaves his desk until his paperwork is caught up, either every day or every Friday, will never get far behind. But unfortunately, most editors are too busy to be this together. Generally, you should hear reasonably quickly about totally rotten ideas. The first person reading your letter will know that you're way off base and will probably just toss your query to some secretary to return immediately.

Likewise, queries containing perfectly fabulous ideas are also generally (but not always!) answered quickly. The editor doesn't want to take the chance of one of his competitors beating him to this wonderful article, so he will generally act quickly.

Unfortunately, probably 90% of all article ideas are neither totally rotten nor totally fabulous. Most are somewhere in the middle, and an absolute decision on their fate cannot be made quickly.

Some magazine editors put a huge chart on the wall with space for each issue for the next year or longer. As good ideas come in and articles are assigned, they're slotted into the appropriate spaces. As each issue gets filled, that's it. Once they're all filled, no new ideas are needed or wanted until they start the chart for the next year.

Some magazines, generally but not always quarterlies and bi-monthlies, plan more than a year in advance too—but they slot in all the articles at one time. That means that if you happen to send in your query right after they've planned all the issues for the next year (and this does not always happen on a regular calendar year), you're out of luck until nine months or so down the road when they start planning for the next year's issues.

I would hazard a guess that most magazines work about five or six months in advance. That means that they're looking over Christmas ideas in June or July, and can only choose from amongst the Christmas ideas they **have** in June or July. (Keep this in mind—always send in your seasonal ideas at least six months in advance. Better to be early than late.)

So let's say it's June. All of the editors get together for a big long meeting to plan that all-important Christmas issue, generally the biggest issue of the year, especially for consumer magazines. Of course, most of the ideas that have been sent in in the past month or so have not been Christmas ideas, they've just been general ideas. (Most people just cannot get into the spirit in May!) But each editor has a list of ideas he or she thinks may be appropriate, and is prepared to sell them to everybody else. Once you are in close with one editor, you may be told when one of your special ideas is going to be brought up at a story meeting.

Let's say that 50 good ideas are brought up at this meeting, but there is only room for 22 articles. Maybe a few of the extras will be dismissed, but many will be "carried over" until the next meeting, for the January issue. In the meantime, of course, a lot of new general ideas come in, and the leftover December ideas have to compete all over again against them in July (for January).

So I think you can see how some ideas can hang around an editor's office for a long time. If he really believes in your idea, and really wants the article in the magazine, he may hang in there, bringing it up again and again at four or even six meetings (or more). Only seldom will he write or call and tell you that they're "still thinking about it". But after two months or so you have a perfect right to wonder what has happened.

Of course, check your market books before you take any action. Some editors will have very honestly reported there that they take six months (or more) to respond to queries.

Some writers only wait three weeks before sending a follow-up letter, but I believe that is too short a time. Some writers never follow up at all—they just assume they've been rejected if they don't hear anything within a reasonable amount of time, say three to six months.

I recommend that you do follow up on any queries you send out if you don't have an answer after about two months. (This is assuming that you've sent an SASE—if you didn't, you can rightly expect to not have an answer.)

Keep a record of your queries. Two methods I have used both worked fine. One is to have an index card for each idea, the other is to have a page in a notebook for each idea (this is better, as there is more room to write). Record just enough information so that you know exactly which idea and approach you're referring to at the top of the page or card. Then record each magazine you've sent the idea to, the name of the editor, and the date. Leave an additional column for the answer—rejection or acceptance. A record like this only takes a few minutes to keep up each time you send out a query, and will really come in handy. It's a snap to check off returned ideas, and then decide where to send them next. If you have dozens or even hundreds of different ideas circulating at all times, you might have trouble keeping them straight.

With a record like this, you can also see at a glance which ideas are still "outstanding", and then decide when to follow up on them.

This record will also come in handy if the tax people should come calling. You're generally able to deduct home business expenses only if you can prove that your writing is a business and not your hobby. By showing them that you are seriously looking for work—via your record of hundreds of queries—your case is strengthened.

I have seen books that contain record sheets for writers, but they consist of generally just one long list. This would be okay if you only send out a couple of queries a month, but if you have dozens of ideas all over the place all the time, it would be totally inadequate. Each time you wanted to send out a query you'd have to look through the whole record book to find out where it's been. If you make your own book and index it by idea, you'll save yourself a lot of time.

If I haven't heard from an editor after two months I drop him a short note, simply asking if he got my query. (Things truly do get lost in the mails occasionally.) Mention briefly the ideas you sent in—just a sentence or two each—to jog his memory. (You can't expect him to remember everybody's ideas.) Mention the date the query was mailed too, as some editors keep files by dates, and be sure to enclose another SASE with this letter.

If you don't hear anything within another three or four weeks, then you have a choice. You can just wait indefinitely, just forgetting about that idea for the time being. Yes, it does happen occasionally that you get a note out of the blue more than a year later—sometimes a rejection but sometimes an assignment for the article—it's happened to me at least a dozen times.

If it's a great idea that you're anxious to do, you may not want to wait. In this case, I would send a third letter with either a photocopy of the second one, or again outline the ideas you are inquiring about. (The second letter may have gotten lost. Don't ever put complete faith in the mail system of any country.) Don't be upset or rude—just ask nicely if he's a) received, and/or b) made a decision on your idea. Enclose still another SASE. And at the bottom of this letter, say something like this: "If I do not hear from you by (mention the date three or four weeks hence), I will assume you are not interested in this idea and will send it elsewhere".

Note this date in your record book, and when the date has passed, feel free to submit the idea to somebody else. If the original editor calls and asks for the article before anyone else shows any interest in it, then you're still free to do the article for him if you want to.

Most writers wonder about sending out simultaneous queries—that is, sending out the same article ideas to different magazines at the same time. There are two equally valid sides to this argument.

Many writers and most editors feel that this should never be done, and I can understand their reasons perfectly. Because it does frequently take time for a magazine to decide on any given article, they feel that they should have the right to expect exclusivity to the ideas they receive until they make their decision. Often magazines run groups of articles that are tied together in some way and would be very upset if they choose yours as one of the pivotal pieces only to find out when they contact you that someone else beat them to assigning you the article. In a case like this you might never be offered an assignment again from the editor you disappointed.

But I can also understand the reasons **for** sending out simultaneous queries.

If you want to make enough money to be able to write full-time you have to write an awful lot of articles—perhaps as many as a couple of hundred a year (depending of course on what each one pays). That means that you cannot wait until you finish one before you look for more work. You must constantly have a lot of queries circulating—maybe as many as forty or fifty at one time.

And while it's easy to come up with ideas, it's not easy to constantly come up with really **good** ideas. No matter how long you've been in the business, most of the ideas you send out will probably still be rejected.

So in order to keep your slate full, you will have to try to find homes for the really good ideas you do come up with as soon as possible. If you send out your space shuttle idea to only one magazine at a time—each of which may take three, four or six months to reply—your idea will be old and gray by the time you sell it. (Or even more likely, someone else will send the same idea to the right magazine at the right time, and you'll be out of luck.)

I do send out simultaneous queries, for the reasons mentioned above. But I try to do it carefully, and I have never been "caught". By this I mean that it has never happened to me that two editors have called and asked for the same article.

You will probably also be all right if you do your simultaneous querying carefully. This means never sending the same idea at the same time to magazines in direct competition—Good Housekeeping and Family Circle, for example. (I'm using names of biggies as examples that everybody will be familiar with—of course you won't be querying magazines like this when you're starting out.)

Let's say you come up with a new way to sprout house plants. You might perhaps want to send this idea to Good Housekeeping, a gardening magazine, and a hobby magazine too. If it's a fabulous idea that you're sure Good Housekeeping will want, then don't send it to anyone else until you've heard from them, even if it takes six months. It's worth the wait because Good Housekeeping pays probably ten times as much as the others, and also because the prestige of having Good Housekeeping on your resume is almost without equal.

On the other hand, you may have an idea on a subject of nutrition that could be adapted to any kind of magazine, and you don't really care that much who publishes it. You just want to get it published as soon as possible, before it's out of date (which frequently happens with health-type ideas). You could then perhaps send it to Good Housekeeping, American Health, and even Playboy, all at the same time—none of these are in direct competition. (So even if all three of them should call you on Monday morning begging for the article, you could still probably write up the idea into three completely different articles slanted to the three different magazines, and please everybody.) If somebody is particularly hot for your idea, he should have the sense to snap it up immediately, and not keep you hanging on.

Editors should know that if they do not answer a letter within a reasonable amount of time—perhaps as little as three weeks—many writers just consider themselves rejected and submit the idea elsewhere anyway without formally withdrawing it. If an editor gets something fabulous, he should have things together enough to know it and act on it immediately. If he does not, then perhaps he deserves to lose out. Of course this does not help your case if an editor gets upset with you when he's the one that loses out.

This question of simultaneous queries is one that is asked of the editors who fill out forms for a listing in the Writer's Market, so be sure to check there. Some will say that it's okay as long as you tell them, so be sure to do so. This will warn them that they'd better act fast if they want your idea, and don't want their competition to have it.

But if the magazine you're interested in is not listed in the Writer's Market, you'll have to make your own decision on this issue. Or even if the magazine is listed, and states that simultaneous queries are perfectly okay, you still may not want to do it—for ethical reasons or because you feel it may work against you. You should weigh this situation carefully before deciding what to do—I cannot tell you what is right for you. If you think you would be incapable of handling the job of telling an editor that you're sorry, but someone else asked for a particular article first, then don't send out simultaneous queries. You'll just have to have forty or fifty **different** ideas circulating at all times!

I'd like to put in a word here about persistence. Even in the prime of my career I have had times when I had fifty ideas all turned down in a row, and times when I really had nothing to do because all of my queries had been rejected.

Sometimes I come up with such fabulous incredible ideas and get all excited about them—only to have them all rejected, over and over again. I absolutely cannot understand why sometimes. I thought for months about the last three ideas I sent to Cosmopolitan, my favorite magazine. I thought they were absolutely perfect—but they were still rejected.

If this happens to people like me—and believe me, it does—it will certainly happen to you when you're starting out. It will be hard at times for you to not get discouraged, I know. Sometimes the sheer disappointment may make you want to chuck it all and go back to working in the laundry.

I can suggest two things. First, be absolutely sure that your query letters are perfect—that you have professional stationery, perfect grammar, spelling and punctuation, and that your typewriter and your typing are well above average. If everything really is perfect in that regard, take a second look at your ideas. Are you sure they're fresh and appropriate for the places you're sending them? Are you contacting magazines in your league? You may just not be considered experienced enough yet for the caliber of magazines you're contacting—try going back to some new or smaller magazines for a while.

If you can honestly say that all of these things are not the problem, then you'll just have to try to hang in there. Remember that it took six months before I got a single assignment from my weekly query letters back in 1983, and I'm sure there's more competition now.

When most people get discouraged they tend to slack off. But I'd like to suggest to you that when things look dark try sending out **more** letters, not less—try ten a week, or twenty. Whatever you do, don't give up. There's so much work out there, it is truly only a matter of time before you hook up with somebody who needs you. But you'll never make it if you quit.

Even if you're only able to come up with ten good ideas, keep sending those ten out, again and again. If you give up after only one or two tries, I can guarantee that you'll never make it.

But you can really make it if you hang in there.

A special note about new magazines. If you use the methods outlined in a later chapter of this book for finding new magazines, you may be writing to some of them before they've had even one issue out. In this case, your query must of necessity be looser. If you can judge from the title of the magazine what it is going to be like—Space Shuttles Unlimited!— you may be able to come up with some appropriate ideas. Or if you get a chance to talk with the editor before you write, you can ask what sort of things he is looking for.

If you know nothing, you can always just be enthusiastic. "The title (or premise) of your magazine intrigues me—I'd love to do some writing for you! If you'll kindly send me a copy of your guidelines, or let me know the sort of articles you'll be looking for, I'll rush you some ideas." Just use your own judgement here. In some cases you may not even have a title or premise or anything. In a case like this you can always rely on the old standard: "I thrive on new challenges!"

If you've spent an afternoon with your *Writer's Market* or *The Writer's Handbook,* you may have found a few magazines that you think you'd like to write for. But many of them may not be available on newsstands, or just may not be available in your city. In a case like this, it's worth the time to write to them for a sample copy and the writer's guidelines, if they have them. If you send in a query based on just what is written in the market books, you may get lucky and hit the nail on the head— but your letter has an equal chance of sounding off-color. An editor can usually tell from your letter if you've read his magazine or not. And if you haven't read it, he will wonder why you want to write for it—and why you think you can. (Pulling a stunt like this will also brand you as lazy—too lazy to write for a copy or to go to a library and look one up—

and this is a bad first impression.) Take the time to at least look at the magazine before you write.

A word here on phoning in queries. Although some editors have told the market books that they don't mind getting telephone queries, don't think that applies to every editor. After all, you may call at the worst possible moment, when he's dealing with his biggest crisis of the day or the month, and his barking "What do you want!?" into the phone is not the nicest way to start a relationship.

I personally feel that, even if an editor states that he is open to phone queries, your **first** contact with him should be by letter. A written query gives you a chance to take your time and plan carefully what you're going to say, and it gives him a chance to look over a sample of your work—your letter. He will see at a glance how professional it looks, how confident and professional you come across. (If you're nervous on the phone, it won't come across very well at all.) Never forget that your writing is your most important and valuable product—it should always be presented in the best possible light. If you come across badly on the phone, a later letter may not change the editor's opinion of you.

And on top of that, even if you do talk with an editor who doesn't know you well—he's going to tell you to "put it in a letter for me" anyway!

After you've worked with an editor a couple of times you can ask if it's okay to discuss ideas over the phone in the future. When I was an editor I preferred this method for dealing with writers I knew because it saved a lot of time and paperwork—and I know many other editors feel this way too. (Remember that possibly 90% of the ideas a magazine gets will be rejected anyway—that can be done in only a second on the phone.) This will more likely be the case with writers who live in the same city where the magazine is published—relationships tend to be closer in a situation like this. If you write for a magazine regularly, even if it's thousands of miles away, a phone call (or occasional personal meeting) can get so much done so much faster.

I used to write two articles per month for one trade magazine. We would spend about a half-hour on the phone together every third or fourth month. He would give me some assignments, and I would suggest some ideas from a running list I kept. We would work everything out, I would send off the contracts, and then he would leave me on my own to do the articles and see that he got them by the various deadlines. I would go about my work, and only let him know if I was having some kind of problem, or if I ran into some topic that was current and should be done immediately. For example, once I got the opportunity to have a meeting with the prosecuting attorney in a case of great importance to the audience of this magazine. I called the editor to make sure he wanted the article before I wasted the attorney's time, and my own.

Remember that even if you are an old and trusted contributor, even if you write a column, you'll probably have to have all of your topics approved before you can go ahead—the whole magazine has to have some kind of continuity, you know. This sort of thing is usually taken care of with a phone call (or even lunch). Only a few editors will insist on having every idea written down in detail when you're a constant contributor. The exception to this is when you're dealing with a really big magazine, where ideas are discussed at story meetings with several other editors or higher-ups. In cases like this your editor will generally have to have something in writing to present to the others at the meeting.

But you'll know that you have an editor's absolute confidence and trust when he will approve four or ten ideas ahead of time, tell you the deadlines, and then seemingly forget about you. There are not that many writers who can be counted on in this way—and editors constantly pray for their good health. Be sure that the editors you work for know that you can be counted on in this way, right from the beginning. It's a big part of being a professional.

Even if you've never been published before, your professionalism can show through in your letter. If your letter is clean and clear, this speaks volumes about you and the way you work. Editors are editors because they have a lot of experience. They can tell at a glance if you know what's happening, if you're a good writer, and if you'd (probably) be able to handle an assignment. Make your query letters as good as they can possibly be—they will impress the heck out of editors who are used to receiving "junk mail" from so-called writers.

If you keep getting printed rejection slips—you know the ones—"This just doesn't suit our needs at this time, but thank you for thinking of us!"—there is probably something wrong with your approach.

It's possible that three or five editors may have been blind about recognizing your obvious talent and good ideas, but not a whole bunch of them. If you get twenty or more of those printed rejections in a row, you might want to think about changing your approach. Start by having someone read the copies of the letters you've been sending out, to see if he or she can spot the problem.

If your letters are good but the ideas just aren't quite right, many times you will get a personal note from the editor or someone—even if it's only scribbled on the bottom of the printed rejection form. (I've reached this stage with Cosmopolitan.) There are generally only two occasions that would find you getting dozens of printed rejections to your queries in a row—when you've only been querying some of the many magazines that never do business any other way, or when something is really turning people off. (You can quite rightly expect them if you send out only unsolicited manuscripts.) Go over your letters and see if you can find out what may be turning everybody off. Bad typing? Strikeovers? Grammar or punctuation mistakes? Old stale unoriginal ideas? Too much bragging or complaining?

Keep your letters clean, businesslike and professional—and your ideas appropriate and fresh—you won't lose with an approach like that.

GETTING ALONG
WITH YOUR EDITOR

Some things in this chapter have been mentioned briefly elsewhere in this book, but I want to bring everything together here because this is one of the most important aspects of writing for a living. If you do not get along with your editors on a long-term, continuing basis, you are o-u-t. Like any other group of people, some editors are wonderful and some are miserable. Most fall in between, with good days and bad days, usually determined by the schedule of the magazine they're working on. (If it's two days til they go to press, it's a very, very bad day.)

But there are a few general guidelines you should always follow when dealing with editors. Although they are not our "bosses" in the strict sense of the word—we're our own bosses when we freelance—we still depend on them to give us work. If you are not easy or nice to work with, sooner or later you will have alienated all of the editors you may get work from— and that will be the end of your career.

If a particular editor is truly impossible to get along with—and some are—you have to decide if it is worth it to you to keep writing for his magazine. If the pay is acceptable and you love the work you get from that magazine, you can certainly put up with more than if you hate it. If it's bad news all around, take your tearsheets and move on. If you've done good work for him, no matter how he treated you, the tearsheets will be good and you can use them to find other work. These copies of your articles will speak for you—you don't have to get a reference or anything from your former editors.

If you want to stay, however, you can try to work around the editor. This happened to me once. We got into a disagreement of some kind each time I saw him, so I started mailing in my stories instead of taking them in in person, or I went only when I knew he wouldn't be there. He didn't mind my calling, so I got my assignments over the phone. He obviously liked my work, as he kept giving me a lot of assignments, but we just really didn't get along.

Of course the best thing to do is simply to let it all roll off your back. You never really know what kind of pressure your editors are under—

and theirs is a very demanding job. Don't forget that some editors may be unpleasant to you on occasion simply because they envy you—they may wish they could be free to (or have the guts to) freelance like you do.

But if you follow all of these guidelines, along with common sense manners, chances are good that you won't get anybody upset with you. Be considerate right from the very beginning. Most editors will tell you that a good percentage of writers do not do these things that follow. If you do, he will probably treat you especially well because he won't want to lose you. (Yes, these things really are that important!)

1. Remember that editors are extremely busy people, especially at medium-to-large magazines. You wouldn't believe how busy they are. So give them a break.

Don't call unless an editor has told you specifically that he wants you to call, or it's something vitally important. And when you do call, speak with his assistant or secretary first—tell her why you're calling and she might be able to take care of you without bothering him, or at least pass along your message when she knows that things are relatively calm. For example, if you're calling to make an appointment to come in to discuss ideas with an editor you've worked with before, there's no need to speak to him personally. The secretary can schedule your appointment. Or she may call back and tell you that he's asked that you send him a letter with the ideas first, before coming to the office.

This may sound a little silly to you, but consider what might happen if every writer called the editor all the time. Most magazines keep stables of at least 50-100 semi-regular writers, and sometimes more—and then there are all those new people always trying to break in. If everybody called, the editor would never have any time for his real work—putting together the magazine.

Try to learn the schedule of the magazine—the secretary can generally tell you this. Especially important is knowing when they go to press so that you can avoid all business during that time. Unless you've edited a magazine, or witnessed those last few hectic days, you have no idea what it's like then.

Don't assume that just because a magazine is very small that the editor has less to do. At many small magazines the editor is not only an editor, but also the chief sales rep and the main distributor. So just ask if he wants you to keep in touch by phone—many of them do. Some editors are so insecure that they want twice-weekly (or even daily) reports on any article you're doing for them.

But of course there are times when you really must call—times when something is vitally important. If you call to ask the editor if you should interview three doctors or four for your next article, or ask where you can find a certain reference volume, or to check the word length of an assignment—these things simply brand you as incompetent. If you continually bother an editor with questions like these, you'll quickly become a royal pain and may not get any more work from that magazine. (Never forget that there are a lot of eager young people out there just waiting to jump into your shoes and take your assignments.)

Once you're "in" with a magazine, don't take it for granted. If you are a real professional, act like one. The editor will think there is something wrong with you if you keep asking dumb questions—either by phone or in letters. A real professional knows the assignment before he accepts it (see the chapter on Getting The Assignment), and certainly knows how to do his own research.

Some things, however, **are** vitally important. Always notify the editor if you won't be able to keep your deadline, if you won't be able to handle the assignment at all, if you simply cannot do an article the way you agreed to and time is running short, or if something spectacular has happened and you can offer him a "scoop".

It is much better to call and admit it if you cannot make a deadline than to just wait and turn in your article late, figuring or hoping that the editor won't notice. You may not realize this, but magazines are on very strict and important schedules, and even one day, even 12 hours late can throw things off like you wouldn't believe. Magazines have to reserve time at a busy printer's, and if the stuff is not ready and there on time the schedules of perhaps dozens of other people who use that printer are upset.

If you absolutely cannot make a deadline, for whatever reason, call as soon as possible—the minute you know you won't be able to make it—and tell the editor. He will then decide if he can wait a few extra days, reschedule your article for another issue, or scrap it altogether. Sometimes he will be able to wait, because he has wisely given his writers a deadline that is a little inflated, one that allows for problems.

Don't wait until the very last minute to call if you know you can't make the deadline. (And this goes double for ploys like just not turning in the manuscript and then acting dumb when somebody calls you and asks where it is. Every editor has heard, at least ten times: "It must have gotten lost in the mail!") If you let an editor down in this way, even once, you may never get another assignment from him or any of his friends. (Yes, editors do have lunch together and occasionally talk about their writers.) There are simply too many writers out there for any editor to take a chance on you again after you've done something like this.

But editors are human (yeh, really!), and do understand if you get sick, if your grandfather dies, etc. All they ask is that you give them as much notice as possible to reschedule. Wise editors have what's called a "bank", a file full of completed articles that are all edited and ready to go, in case something happens to a regularly scheduled piece. But many magazines cannot afford to keep a bank, and some just don't want to be bothered. Some have a small group of freelancers that they know they can depend on 100%, and who work fast. If an article falls through, they might call one of these contingency players and ask if he or she is free to do an article in three days (or one). This has happened to me several times, because editors know that they can always count on me when they're in a spot. Try to get that reputation for yourself.

More than likely, your article will just be moved to a future issue and something from the bank will be used to fill its space. Only when an article is very timely or seasonal will it have to be scrapped. (Christmas only comes once a year.)

When I edited a magazine, I gave each writer a different deadline, so that the articles came in one at a time, which was all I could work on anyway. Since somebody always turned in his or her article early, it really didn't matter if one was late—I just planned to do it last (assuming it wasn't **too** late). But not every editor has organized a system like this, and many do not allow at all for problems.

So to avoid any potential problems even if you should get sick or your grandfather die, plan your writing time so that you'll have your article ready at least a week before it's due. Then if something does happen, you're covered. Be especially careful if you've been entrusted with the cover story or something else equally important. Always try to get this type of article done as early as possible, as it would ruin the whole issue, including the cover photo, if this article was not delivered. Then you'd really be in trouble!

2. As with the phone calls above, never drop in on an editor uninvited. If you want to come in and go over some ideas in person rather than in a letter (only do this if you've worked with an editor before), make an appointment. In many cases you will find that you get more work from an editor if you do go in in person occasionally. Maybe he's too guilty to turn you down when you're sitting right across from him, but more likely you're just more able to fire up his enthusiasm for an idea if you can pitch it vocally.

Never make an appointment with an editor you've never worked for. Send a letter first, with a few good ideas and tearsheets, and then say something like: "I'd really like to meet you and go over these ideas with you. Just give me a call—I'm free to meet with you anytime at your convenience." If he likes your letter, your ideas, or both, he probably will want to meet you. It's always nice to know who you're dealing with.

If you're making a trip to New York or wherever some of your magazines are, and would like to meet some editors you've worked for while you're there, send your requests for appointments as far in advance as possible. You may be able to line up all the visits. You'll find that this is an excellent thing to do because an editor will tend to think of you more often if you've met (and you've made a good impression). For the same reason, always send Christmas cards to every editor you've worked with. (I usually take batches of cookies to the ones in town.) Keep in touch. Remember, there are an awful lot of writers asking these guys for work constantly, and most of them will be unknown. If an editor can flip through his pile of mail and spot a letterhead from somebody he knows, he will probably read that letter first.

Never forget that it is repeat work from magazines you've already done something for that will make your writing career a full-time one!

3. Really listen to what your editor says. You'd be surprised (astonished) to learn how many writers don't do this. Always take notes when speaking, in person or on the phone. He will give little hints and tips about what he wants or the way he wants things done whenever you talk. Be sure that you get them all down. He may not even remember saying some things to you, but will be truly amazed when you hand one of his own ideas right back to him. In fact, he may think that you think exactly like he does, and will give you loads of work.

So listen to him. If he says he wants your article to be 1200 words, he means it. Not 1000, and not 2200. It takes quite a while to cut or add to someone else's work. The editor gives you a word length for a reason—because he has only so much room in the magazine for your article—so write down what he says and stick to it. Magazines are generally planned months in advance, and filling the pages is almost like putting a jigsaw puzzle together. There's generally a big chart with spaces for each page, and the ads are placed in as they're contracted for. The articles then have to be fitted in between and around those ads. It's a big job, especially at large magazines that may have 20 or more articles and columns in each issue. It can get very complicated.

Occasionally an article you're working on will get so involved, or you'll just find so much stuff to write about that you can't even begin to select what is best. In a case like this, call the editor. If it's all really fabulous stuff, he may tell you to go ahead and double the length. He can push some other article into a later issue to find room, or he may have you make yours into a two-parter. If he really doesn't want more than the originally-assigned 1200 words, he can tell you what aspect you should focus on and what you should leave out.

But if it's a case of going over by only a couple of hundred words, it's generally okay. But be sure to mention in a covering letter that you have gone a bit over, and by how much, so that he can read the article with an eye towards cutting it if the space allowed is inflexible.

Actually, many editors really wouldn't mind having a few extra words to "play with". Most writers sometimes get "wordy", and it's usually not hard to find something to cut or condense. Reader's Digest, for example, routinely asks for an extra 500-1000 words on an original article so that they can form it the way they want.

Writing **less** than you're supposed to, however, is another matter. It's quite difficult to add a half-dozen paragraphs without doing an additional interview or some additional research, and believe me, editors do not have time for that sort of thing. If you just can't seem to stretch the article out without becoming obvious about it (and "stretching" is a bad practice anyway), then **you** need to do an additional interview or some more research. If an article looks obviously padded it gives a very poor impression.

But padded or shorter than needed, you will probably just get the article back to rewrite. Save yourself this hassle by just doing it right in the first place. There is no such thing as a story that can't be made longer. All you need is to find one more person to interview.

And also, if an editor tells you that he wants you to take a certain approach with an article, even if you think it's wrong and/or dumb, do it anyway. He has a reason for asking for what he wants. (Perhaps the magazine has to have a certain article in a certain way in a certain issue in order to attract certain advertisers. This is done often.) If you don't understand exactly what he wants, ask again—until you really understand. Never leave an editor's office or hang up a phone until you're totally sure of your assignment. If you don't do the article right, it's generally assumed to be your fault.

Many editors routinely send out letters of assignment for each article that is commissioned. It tells exactly what he wants, perhaps in outline form, how you should do it, if there are any particular people you should be sure to interview, and anything else you need to know—like what you'll be paid, and the deadline. If your magazines are not in the practice of using assignment letters, see if you can get them to do it for you anyway. It's an excellent idea, and makes for a lot less misunderstanding all around. In many ways assignment letters are even better than contracts, because they go into much more detail. Lucky are you if you hook up with a magazine that sends out both!

You will occasionally run across editors who are simply not good at explaining what they want from you. They know in their minds what they want, but just cannot put it properly into words. But upon reading what you turn in, it only takes them a second to see that it's not at all what they wanted.

What can you do in a case like this? (It's happened to me a few times too. Even the most experienced and competent writers cannot avoid this kind of situation completely.)

Ideally you will have an assignment letter from the editor, and you can show him in black and white that you did what he asked for. But that probably won't let you off the hook completely. I had an editor once that I could not, no matter how much I tried, convince that what he was asking for **now** was a totally different article than what he asked for before —and I even had an outline from his own little typewriter.

But in any case—if it is your fault, or his fault for not being able to explain what he wanted adequately—he is still entitled to a rewrite. It's best just to offer to do it and not make a fuss. You are generally required to do one rewrite for no additional pay. But if he wants an entirely different article that would encompass a lot of extra new research and interviews, you are entitled to ask for some extra money. Of course this doesn't mean that you'll get it—especially if it was your fault that the article wasn't done properly or thoroughly enough in the first place. However, if you can convince him that he just changed his mind about what he wanted after he saw what you turned in—and this happens more than anybody would like to know—then you should rightly get some extra money.

You can protect yourself from this sort of thing somewhat by always reading back to the editor, from your notes, what you understand the assignment to be. Or you can write him a letter, stating in detail what you understand the assignment to be—while there is still time enough to get a correction if you're a little off base. (I highly recommend this the first time you work with a new editor. You don't know if he will turn out to be one of those who cannot clearly explain what he wants you to do.) On the bottom of this letter state that if you do not hear otherwise from him within 7-10 days (give the specific date) you will assume that your view of the assignment is correct.

If you go ahead and do an article without ascertaining that it is 100% what the editor wants, then it may not be accepted and you will have wasted your time. Some articles are so specific that you simply cannot sell them anywhere else.

This is a good place to talk about "kill fees". You should always inquire about kill fees when you accept your first assignment from a publication, and they should be spelled out in your contract and/or assignment letter.

Now not every magazine pays kills fees, and many which do have their own system. However, the following is generally considered by writers groups as being ethical and fair:

a) You're entitled to a 100% kill fee (the total amount you were promised for an article plus expenses the magazine agreed to pay) if your article is not accepted or published when it is absolutely not your fault. There are several occasions when this might happen. The owners of a magazine may decide to cease publication. They may decide to scrap that planned special real estate issue because they can't get enough advertisers. They may sell too much advertising and have to bump a couple of articles. If this happens with a Christmas issue, for example, obviously they can't just stick the articles in the next issue.

In all of these instances, and those similar, you're rightfully entitled to full payment for the work you did. If you failed to ask about this before you accepted an assignment, you can still try to get the money afterwards if something like this happens—but you may not get anything. (Some publishers who pay only on publication will adamantly hold to their stand that if it's never published, it should never be paid for.) It's always better to ask about a magazine's policy before you need to know it.

If you are having trouble negotiating a kill fee with an editor, try using this example, which is easier for most people to understand than the writer's dilemma: If you commission an artist to paint a picture for you, and then later on you decide not to hang it—you still owe the artist something for his time.

b) When you take an assignment also be sure you inquire about a magazine's policy for partial kill fees. Some will be 10% or less, some a respectable 50% or even more. This will be the amount you are entitled to if it is basically your fault if the article is unacceptable and/or unpublishable.

Some articles come in so badly researched and so badly written that it is pointless even to ask for a rewrite. The writer is just obviously incompetent, or unable to handle that particular assignment, and even a rewrite wouldn't help that article. In some cases, this can be the editor's fault. He should have given the assignment "on spec" if he was unsure of a writer's qualifications to handle an assignment. (This is, of course, the main reason editors prefer to work with experienced writers—so they can see some samples and know that you're capable before they give you an assignment.)

But even if you turn in a totally unusable article, you are still entitled to a little something for your time (unless you worked on spec). This little something is the partial kill fee. When you're paid a partial kill fee you immediately get the rights back to your article, and you can sell it somewhere else that very same day (if you can). And you don't have to tell the new magazine that it's been rejected by someone else.

It is important to know the magazine's policy on partial kill fees before you start working on an article, and they should be in writing somewhere, either in your contract or your assignment letter. People can have conveniently short or faulty memories, and after an article has been rejected is no time to be fighting over a kill fee.

4) The last point in getting along with your editor is simple: be loyal. That's an old-fashioned word, but it's a quality you should develop if you don't

have it. In essence, it means not spreading gossip or rumors (even if true) about the magazines and the editors you work with.

This only really becomes a problem if you start writing for several different magazines at the same time, or two or more in the same field. Some editors will try to pump you for information about their rivals, but you should be very careful. If you get branded as a gossip, or a spy, you may not get much work.

A part of the magazine world is getting scoops and stories ahead of your competition. And in some cases, with certain magazines, this competition can get very cut-throat. All I'm saying is that you should try to stay out of the middle of this sort of thing.

Now I realize that even if you write for a lot of magazines, one will be your "favorite". You may be tempted to tell the editor what his competition is doing, if you know. Just remember that all of those magazines pay your salary, and even if some of them treat you better than others, all should get equal loyalty from you. It will pay off in the long run.

GETTING THE ASSIGNMENT

If your query letter has been looked favorably upon, you'll be getting a call or a letter from the editor. If it's a call, and you're within easy travelling distance, ask if you can come in to discuss the assignment in person. It's easier to work with someone that you've met, and you'll find that the editor feels the same way.

If the magazine is far away you'll have to do most of the negotiating by letter—unless the magazine is rich and prefers to conduct business over the phone. (Some will even tell you that you can call collect—that's truly a sign of a rich magazine!)

The first meeting with an editor is usually a bit nerve-wracking, especially if it's a magazine you're dying to get into. By all means, dress up—a suit and a tie if you're a man, a dress or nice skirt and blouse if you're a woman. First impressions are always important. If you look neat and serious, your chances of getting an assignment from the editor skyrocket.

Carry an attaché case or neat folder or envelope if you're bringing along samples or written ideas. Stay away from plastic tote bags, brown paper sacks, etc. If you truly look like a professional, you'll be considered one, and treated like one. The last thing you want to do is to be branded as an amateur, even before you open your mouth.

Be sure that you're on time—15 minutes early is even better. That will give you time to sit for a minute and compose yourself. If it's a big magazine, watching the bustle around you will psych you up. But be loose— many times the person you have the appointment with will be running late. Just smile and tell the receptionist that you have all day. Ask for a couple of back issues of the magazine to read while you're waiting— this is a nice touch. Never just sit there fidgeting.

Chances are good that the secretary or receptionist is a close friend of the editor's, so be careful what you say. Don't start asking her for a bunch of gossip, or ask her how to "soften up the editor", or tell her that this is the first time you've ever visited a magazine or met an editor (even if it is). Whatever you say to anyone you meet there may very well get back to the editor after you're gone—and it may even get back to him before he meets with you—so be pleasant with everybody. A smile goes a long way.

Before you leave, say good-bye personally to anybody that you've been introduced to, and to the receptionist and secretary. The more friends that you have at a magazine, especially if it's a biggie, will be to your advantage. Yes, it's really true—you will get more work from them if they **like** you!

Be safe and don't schedule any other appointments for a few hours after this one. The editor may be running late, or you may just get talking about something and end up spending a couple of hours together. When you're in an editor's office, don't keep looking at your watch—make him feel that he is the most important person in your whole life at that moment. Actually, he may be.

You will probably already have a reasonably good idea of what he will want to talk to you about before you go in. When he calls you he'll probably say if he wants to get more details on an idea you've already sent in, or if he just wants to toss random ideas around with you. Or he may have a specific assignment all ready and waiting for you!

If he needs more details on a topic you've proposed, really be prepared. If he just wants to discuss ideas, bring a lot of them along. You don't have to bring them all out, but have them ready. Once I had an appointment with an editor of a national glossy I was dying to write for. I took along 20 ideas, which I thought were more than enough. (In fact, I thought they were all wonderful.) But it was only the very last one that piqued the editor's interest. If I had only brought the first 10, or even the first 15, I wouldn't have walked out of her office with an assignment. You just never know what they will want.

Of utmost importance is your flexibility. Whatever the editor suggests, let him know that you can handle it. Some ideas that editors come up with—or some approaches to your ideas—are downright strange. If you think something won't work you can express an alternative approach—but never come out and say something like "why would you want it that way?" or "huh?"

Try to be very diplomatic at all times. Remember that he's in charge of his magazine, not you. Especially if you're just starting out, you may not have much to say about what you write or even how you'll write it. But if you want to get more work from that editor, it's important to be enthusiastic about whatever he wants.

Never leave the office until you understanding everything. If the assignment he gives you is his idea or yours, be sure that you know exactly how he wants it done. If you don't understand something, ask. If you waste your time doing an article the wrong way it will be your own fault. Be sure that you know all the details.

To be very sure, write everything down. Especially if you're excited about the meeting and getting the assignment, you may forget. So take down as much as possible of what he says. It's an excellent idea to bring along a steno pad for this purpose whenever you go to visit an editor. Never put yourself into a position of having to ask him for some paper or a pen. He wants writers who have it all together.

Some editors are obviously better at disclosing what they want than others, so you'll have to listen carefully and get down as much as you can. Try to note key phrases at least. Most editors will give away a lot of clues about things you should include, people you should interview, etc. Ideally, a good set of notes could almost be considered a rough outline of your article. But don't bring along a tape recorder when you attend these meetings—that's going a little too far.

Before you leave the editor's office, be sure that you've understood all the basics. Know exactly what the article is to be about, and which approach you should take. Know if it should be in the first or second or third person, and how formal the writing should be. Know if he wants a lot of quotes or none. Know the length, and how much and when you'll be paid. Know the story on kill fees and which rights the magazine usually buys. Above all, know the deadline.

It's an excellent idea to ask the editor to send you a follow-up (assignment) letter, containing all the information above. This way, there won't be any misunderstanding. Most editors will do this if you ask. Some send printed contracts, but these usually only give a brief sketch of the article, or only the title. An editor who sends out detailed assignment letters usually gets more of exactly what he wants from his writers. In any case, he will be impressed that you've asked for one; it shows that you're a professional.

It's important that you start thinking of yourself as a businessperson, right from the beginning, because that is exactly what you are when you freelance. You own your own little writing business. (And if you're really good, someday it may be a very big business.)

It is unfortunate, and I hate bringing this up, but some magazines do not deal with writers in an entirely honest way. So in addition to asking for an assignment letter to guarantee that you understand the assignment correctly, you should insist on using a contract to protect yourself from unscrupulous publishers. Again, this is a part of being in business. Contracts are an accepted form of doing business these days, and you should never let an editor put you down for asking for one. In some cases, it will be the editor who protests the loudest about how you don't trust him who will cheat you first. It's happened to me.

I don't know exactly why, but some magazines which would never think of putting off paying the electric bill, the printer, or even the people who clean the office, will try to get out of obligations with writers without a moment's hesitation. Don't they realize that without writers they will not have a magazine at all? I think part of it is that some magazines consider writers to be a totally disposable commodity. By this I mean that there are always hundreds or thousands of writers hanging around who will gladly even work for nothing, just to get published.

Now smart editors and publishers will realize that you really get what you pay for in this business, and that if you get people to write for free, a good deal of the time the stuff will be inadequately done, unusable, or just not to professional standards. (The people who write for free are those who cannot get paying assignments.)

But in any case, there are some crooks and cheats around, and it is vital that you protect yourself with a contract these days. I never used a contract until one time I couldn't get my money and had to sue a magazine for $1800. After that, which I won by the way—I could prove that the articles were published and he couldn't prove that he paid me—I never did anything without a contract. However, even though I refused to work without contracts, I have still have had to sue five other people for non-payment. It's a pain to have to go to court, and very stressful even if you're right, but it's easy to win your case when you have a signed contract. If I hadn't had the contracts, I probably wouldn't have won everything I was entitled to.

This all happened to me when I was very experienced, so you can imagine how some unethical people might try to take advantage of newcomers. I cannot stress enough that you must insist on a contract.

There's a basic, simple contract at the end of this chapter. You should type up a good copy on your letterhead and then have a few photocopied. As you accept each assignment, inform the editor that you'll be sending him a contract. Don't ask if it's okay—just tell him that you're sending one, and that you can't do the article until you have it back with his signature. Send him two copies, one for him to sign and keep, and one for him to sign and send back to you (send an SASE to make it easy for him).

Now some editors will refuse to sign a contract. If he makes a real fuss, you should think twice about accepting work from him. When you're starting out you might be willing to take the chance, but once you have plenty of work you should not consider this kind of gamble. If he refuses to sign a contract, there's a reason!

A good thorough assignment letter will probably stand up in court if it gives all the terms and is signed, but a contract is so much more straightforward.

If you cannot get anything in writing from an editor, but still decide to take the chance of writing for him, you can reasonably protect yourself in a simple way. When you get home, immediately type a letter to the editor. In the letter put everything that you can think of about the assignment. Go into detail on what you understand the assignment to be, the length, the style, the payment, etc. (everything mentioned above). Include information on kill fees and rights—everything. (You should have found out all this stuff when he was giving you the assignment. If you didn't, just put in whatever you can.)

At the bottom of this letter state that you are sending it in lieu of a contract or assignment letter, and that if you don't hear otherwise from the editor within 7-10 days (put in the exact date and year), you will consider that everything in this letter is correct and acceptable to him, and then start work on the assignment. Be sure that your letter is dated and that you keep a copy.

Once the deadline that you gave him has passed you can go ahead and do the article, assuming that what you have noted is correct, and knowing that you are protected. If the editor calls when he gets your letter and screams something at you vaguely reminiscent of "How dare you!", you would be wise to pass on that assignment.

Again, you must use your own judgement. Many times the nicest people and the sweetest talkers will be the first to cheat you, so if something just doesn't feel right, be careful. But of course, you can't always tell. I obviously felt okay about all the six people I had to end up suing—or I wouldn't have taken on the work.

If, when you're starting out, just getting published is more important than getting paid, you may want to take on assignments from people you don't trust. But do try to get something in writing in any case. You won't be sorry.

After you've worked for a magazine regularly for a long time and you know what they expect of you, you may want to stop using the assignment letters, but do not stop using the contracts. One of the people I had to sue paid me perfectly on time for every issue for three years. Then one day I guess he ran out of money or something, and wouldn't pay me.

Again, I'm sorry to have to tell you these things. Many magazines operate on the very edge of bankruptcy, no matter how well they seem to be doing and how plush their offices are, and the writers are usually the first ones to not get paid. Protect yourself.

In some cases the first article you do for a magazine will be done "on spec". That means that they are not committed in any way to pay you for it. If the editor likes it after he sees it, he will buy it—otherwise not. Big magazines will frequently make you do your first article for them this way—even if you've had a lot of things published. They want to make sure that you can do things their way. (And in addition, editors know that just because something has been published with your name on it doesn't mean necessarily that you wrote it like that—your original article may have been torn to shreds and totally rewritten by the other editor.) Then, if they like what you do with this on spec article, you'll get signed contracts for all future assignments.

"On speculation" means just that—you're investing your time in the hope that the editor will like the article enough to buy it. So you should always put a lot of time into it. It's extremely important that your first article for any given magazine be your absolute best work.

If they're impressed with the first piece, chances are good that you'll get another assignment very quickly.

Of course you don't want to let your quality go down with successive articles, but do try to make your first one a superstar.

You should never think that you're "above" working on spec. In many cases it is the only way to break into bigger magazines. No matter how many articles you've had published, never be insulted if somebody asks you to work on spec.

If, for some reason, that magazine rejects the article—it will be so good that you can always sell it to somebody else right away!

How long should you wait to hear from an editor you've done something on spec for? I suggest waiting about the same amount of time you'd wait to hear about a query—about two months. Write a nice letter asking "when" he is planning to publish your article, not "if". If you don't hear anything, write again in another month. He may have just put your article into his bank, and may not have need for it for a year or more—or maybe never.

Of course, if you have agreed to accept payment "on publication", it may be a long time before you see any money in a case like this, if ever. And this is just one of many reasons you should try to get the magazine to agree to pay you "on acceptance". (Lots more about this in the chapter: Let's Not Forget To Talk About Money.)

If what you consider to be an unacceptably long period of time has passed without your article being published—let's say a year—you do have the right to withdraw it if you haven't been paid for it. No magazine should be allowed to deposit a whole bunch of "payment on publication" stuff that they may never use (or pay for) into their bank. It's just not fair to writers, and you should be sure to call them on this if it seems to be happening to you. All the writers will thank you.

Just write the editor a letter explaining that you wrote the article so that it would be published, and you'd like to know his intentions. Tell him that if he is not planning to use it in the near future you would like to withdraw it and submit it elsewhere. Frequently this is enough to remind him that he has your article—which he may honestly have simply forgotten about—and then he may schedule it. Or he may return it. It's a gamble to send a letter like that—but it's dumb to let him hold onto your article forever.

If you have been paid for the article, but it is never published, then you have a different story. What you should do depends on the rights that the magazine bought. If all rights were bought you cannot do anything except maybe remind him once in a while that he has your article and that you'd love to see it published.

If he bought first serial rights, his right to publish may vary. Some magazines feel that if they buy first rights they have the first right to publish —even if it takes them three years (or ten). Many writers, writers groups and magazines adhere to the 12-month rule, which I feel is eminently more fair. (This helps stop editors from commissioning and holding onto stuff forever that they will never publish.) This means that when you are paid, the magazine buys the right to publish the article once within 12 months. If it is not published within 12 months, the rights revert back to you. You are then free to sell the article to someone else, or back to the original editor who commissioned it in the first place. (The assigning editor rightfully has first dibs on it, and you should offer it back to him before trying to sell it elsewhere.) If he plans to publish it later, he must pay you again for another 12 months.

It is not a bad idea to ask the editor the magazine's policy in this area when you accept the first assignment. It will probably never come up—most commissioned articles are indeed published—but it never hurts to be prepared.

A SAMPLE CONTRACT

(Have some of these run off on your letterhead, so that your name, address and phone number will be right there.)

STANDARD CONTRACT

Between _____(writer)_____ and ___(name of magazine)___

For working title: _____

Source of idea: Writer _____ Editor _____

Terms of this publication agreement:

Length of article: _____

Date assigned: _____

Date Due: _____

Projected publication date: _____

Fee: _____

Date of payment: _____

Kill fees: _____

Rights: _____

The publication agrees to pay the writer's expenses for the following:

_____

Not to exceed: _____

The writer shall be notified of acceptance or refusal of this article within two weeks of receipt or of deadline, whichever is later, and payment shall be made within thirty days of receipt of the final manuscript.

We, the undersigned, agree to the terms above.

_____   _____
Writer   Editor

Date: _____   Date: _____

Note: Make two copies and be sure that both are signed; keep one and give the other to the editor.

LET'S NOT FORGET
TO TALK ABOUT MONEY

Some magazines are very successful, and consequently pay their writers very well. They know that they get what they pay for. Other magazines are backed up by big corporations or private investors, and even though they may be small, still pay well. They also know that they get what they pay for. (I once luckily wrote for a little magazine that appeared to be a tax shelter for a bunch of doctors—boy, were they generous!)

But many magazines are struggling. They may have been in business for twenty years, but they're still struggling. They'd love to pay more, love to fill their pages with better articles from better writers, but simply cannot. If a magazine is new, it may have adequate money behind it, but chances are equally good that it does not.

It has been my experience in several cases that a new magazine launches with everything looking good, and pays decently and quickly— for the first two issues. And then everything grinds to a halt, or they simply stop paying the writers. This appears like a case of the publisher borrowing perhaps $40,000-$50,000 to start his magazine, and once that runs out— that's it folks. Poor management or a poor premise kills a lot of new magazines.

Some magazines are struggling so much that they don't pay anything at all. You'll find that a lot of the literary-type and poetry magazines fall into this category. Some will pay in free copies of the issue containing your article or with free subscriptions. But even though they do not pay, they never have a shortage of people who want to write for them. For many people, this is a good and relatively easy way to get their first few things published. (Tearsheets are tearsheets. Editors don't ask if you were paid for previously published stories or articles, but many will be familiar with most of the literary magazines and may know which ones pay and which ones don't—so be honest if asked about it.)

Only you know what you will be willing to accept at the beginning of your career. If you use the methods in a later chapter for finding new magazines that will love and appreciate you, you may just be so happy to have the chance to be published a lot that the money will be secondary— at least in the beginning. And that's okay, there's nothing wrong with that. (My first regular writing job paid only $16 a column—I was thrilled!) While you're still "in the mail room", so to speak, those tearsheets can be much more valuable to you than mere money. (And the better they are, the more they're worth.)

But the time will come when you can rightly expect to be paid for your work, or to be paid more if you settled for peanuts at the beginning. So you have to learn to negotiate about money.

Writers can be paid in several ways. One of the most common is to be paid by the word—perhaps 5 cents a word, or 20 cents a word. Another common method is payment by the article—perhaps $400 for all articles of similar length. Or they may have a range of payments—$50-$200 for articles, generally depending on the length and complexity of the article or the experience of the writer. And then some magazines will negotiate each and every article separately.

I once knew a lady who actually got paid for an article by the hour. Having heard that, I guess I'll believe anything.

If the prices are set, there's usually not too much room for discussion (at least in the beginning). "We pay $200 for your first article for us, and $250 for subsequent articles" is not uncommon. "Everybody gets $175" or "Everybody gets 20 cents a word" is also common. You'll find that prices of columns are usually set, no matter what differing lengths you may turn in—but some are paid by the word. If you're paid a set fee for a column it may be comparably less than you'd get for a feature of the same length in the same magazine—but it's regular work, and you can tell people you're a columnist.

If a magazine has a range of payments, you'll probably start at the very bottom. (Sorry about that.) Some magazines even pay beginners less than the minimum wage they've quoted in the *Writer's Market* or *The Writer's Handbook*. (Not nice, but some do it.) It's probably better not to quibble over the first couple of assignments—but once you've proven yourself it's fair to ask for a little bit more money.

Some magazines, even some bigger ones, have a practice that most writers absolutely hate. They won't give you a definite price when they give you the assignment, saying that they'll pay you "what it's worth" after they see the article. Now, like most people, you would probably put a lot more work into an article if you knew you were getting $700 for it than if you were only getting $175. It's very unfair for an editor to expect you to write your little heart out, only to find out later that he's only going to give you $75 for an assignment that took you three weeks.

But even though this is unfair, some magazines still do it. Perhaps they really want to try to take advantage of people and see just how much they can get for how little (there are always writers hanging around who will gladly write for free, you know). Or perhaps they have been burned just once too often in the past—and unfortunately, you have to pay for the mistakes all the writers before you have made.

Many writers will not write for magazines that work like this. But when you're starting out you may not have any choice. If it's a good assignment from a good magazine it's probably worth your while to take it anyway—at least you'll have the tearsheets. But there's not much recourse later if you feel that you've been taken advantage of.

There are some writers groups that are trying to gain standard rates for articles, partly to put a stop to this sort of exploitation. But there is little that you can do if you're on your own. Consider it a learning experience and move on. (At least you'll have one good tearsheet to show to other editors.)

In a situation like this, however, be absolutely sure that you get something in writing, and that the editor will at least spell out the range of possibilities. I once got an assignment letter from a really big magazine that quoted the possible range as $700-$1200—that's almost double. But at least I had the range in writing, and I advise you to do the same. Don't ever forget that editors are people, and some have faulty memories (honestly or on purpose). Only something in writing will settle a dispute in your favor later on.

Negotiating fees can be tricky, even if you've had a lot of experience. Each time you approach a different magazine, if it's your first sale or your 100th, you still have to talk about money.

You can frequently get some idea of the price range by checking the market listings before you go to talk with the editor, but many magazines are not listed there. Especially with new magazines, you may have to go in totally cold, not having a clue what they will offer.

Some editors are easy—they'll come right out and say: "This is the assignment, and should you choose to accept it, you'll get $300". That's a take-it-or-leave-it assignment from a magazine that has standard rates, and everybody gets the same for similar jobs.

Now there is nothing to stop you from asking for more. If you are very experienced, or have some specialized knowledge of the particular subject, or if the assignment is particularly complicated, I would ask (and explain why). Even if you have no special qualifications, if the rate is really low you can always see if you can get more.

If the editor says that the fee will be $100, and you were hoping that this magazine paid more than that, you can always smile and ask: "How about $125?" It certainly never hurts to try this—you'll probably get a higher fee maybe one-third or even one-half of the time. But if you do try this, make your request only a little bit higher than what the editor offered in the first place. If you ask for double the amount, for example, you'll probably never get it—but if you ask for just a little bit more, there's an excellent chance that he may say "okay".

Even if you can convince the editor that you deserve more money, however, it doesn't mean that he has any more to give you.

But many, if not most, magazines have at least some flexibility about what they can pay. Remember that the money he will be giving you does not come right out of the editor's pocket unless he is also the owner of the magazine. But he usually has to answer to some higher-ups (the publishers) who set the wages. But having said that, I also want you to know that frequently an editor will have some "play" in what he is allowed to pay for any given article, even if he insists that everybody gets paid the same amount. He's generally given a range of fees from the management, and has a bit of freedom within that range. If he really wants you or your special article he may be able to sweeten the pot a little. You'll never know unless you ask.

At the magazine I edited I was given a budget for each issue, and I could spend it in whatever way I wanted. If I got some articles cheap,

I could pay more for others. I don't know how common a practice this is, but I found it very workable.

The most interesting negotiations come with editors who ask: "Well, how much do you want?" when passing out assignments. If you can pull it off with a wink and a big smile, your best answer to that question is: "As much as I can possibly get!" (But don't try that without the smile!)

You'll be way ahead in a negotiation of this sort if you can find out the range of prices before you go in to discuss assignments. But if the magazine is not listed in any of the books or magazines that list markets and what they pay, and you can't find out from anyone else who writes for that magazine, you'll be on your own. (This is another occasion when a writers group can come in very handy—you can usually find someone else who has written for a magazine you're interested in.)

If you've had any other things published, you can always say something like: "Well, I usually get 10 cents a word for this kind of thing", or "Such-and-Such, the same type and size of magazine, paid me $300 for an article of this length".

(Try to avoid saying things like: "I can't afford to work for less than 35 cents a word", or "I won't work for less than 35 cents a word", or "I need $600 for my rent next month", or especially, "The more you give me, the better the article will be". All of this just works against you.)

If you're a relative newcomer, do be careful when you negotiate. You do not want to give the impression of only wanting the assignment because you want or need the money.

I have found personally that the more enthusiasm I can muster up for the magazine in general and the assignment in particular, the easier it is to ask for a few extra bucks—and get them.

Whatever you do, don't look sad or disappointed after the price has been decided. Whatever it is, even if you think it's unfair, offer your hand and say "that's fine" with a smile. After all, it **is** money (many magazines don't pay at all), and it is getting published. If you're good, you'll be moving up to magazines that pay better.

In addition to asking about the amount you'll receive in exchange for your article, you'll also have to ask when you'll be getting your check.

Payment can be made in two main ways—on acceptance or on publication. On acceptance means that the invoice for your fee will be put through as soon as the article has passed inspection, as soon as it's been accepted for publication. This is the best way, so try to talk the editor into paying you this way if it isn't already the magazine's standard policy. Anytime you are promised payment on acceptance you should expect your check within thirty days of the day you turn in the assignment. (This is printed on the sample contract, as this is considered to be the most fair way to be paid. If the editor will not agree to these terms, be sure that you scratch that part out and put in the date when you can expect to receive payment. This is one of the most important parts of the contract—be sure to get this information.)

If the magazine pays only on publication and you cannot change the editor's mind about it, you'll have to decide if you're willing to accept the terms he offers. Many writers refuse to write for magazines that pay on publication. If you agree to it, it may be months and months before you see any money, and you won't have any recourse. (Unfortunately too many magazines feel that "on publication" really means three or more months after publication.)

It has been my personal experience, however, that more magazines pay on publication than on acceptance—so if you decide not to write unless you get paid on acceptance, you may have a harder time finding a lot of work. (But I suppose it depends on which magazines you want to write for—you may be lucky and find a whole bunch of them that pay on acceptance with no problem.)

If you choose to take an assignment with payment on publication, I suggest that you ask the editor exactly which issue your article will be in, and exactly when it will be published (this is considered the day the magazine goes to the printer). Then take this specific date, add thirty days to it, and put this date in the space marked "Date of payment" on the contract. This will protect you if your article doesn't get published when it's supposed to be published. Even if your feature gets bumped from the June issue to next January, you can still insist on payment on the date that appears on the contract—(another reason why the contract is so valuable and important).

Many of my friends charge interest when payment is not made on time in situations like this—and I recently started doing the same. We charge two per cent per month, and send a new invoice every month with the charge added to all outstanding fees. There's no reason you cannot do this. If the editor complains, remind him that he did sign the contract stating that payment would be made on a certain date, and it wasn't.

If you do not use a contract, or do not specify the date of payment in writing anywhere, then you may indeed have to wait forever for your money. Some articles get pushed from issue to issue, maybe for a year or even more, and some end up never published. In a case like this, you have no recourse. If you agreed to payment on publication, you have to wait for publication. (You can see why most writers hate payment on publication.) Of course, if the article is never published you're entitled to a kill fee—but they may not decided to never publish it until three years from now.

The only way around this potential mess is to get a specific date of payment in writing somewhere—anywhere. An assignment letter would be okay if the editor refuses to sign a contract or refuses to write in a payment date on the contract. If he absolutely will not give you a date or allow you to insert one on the contract, or insists on the words "on publication" to be filled in after "Date of payment", you have to decide if you want to take your chances with this assignment.

Payment on publication is considered unfair by almost everybody who writes, and only when every writer flatly refuses to work for magazines that pay this way will we see any changes. (Personally, I don't think that will happen in my lifetime.)

If you cannot get an editor to agree to total payment on acceptance, you should try to get him to agree to pay you half (or at least some part) on acceptance (or even in advance). Try to explain to him that making you wait for the whole payment is unfair. He gets a regular salary paycheck immediately upon finishing each two weeks or one month of work, but as a freelancer, you don't. Remind him that your rent comes due on the first of every month, just like his. But whatever you can get him to agree to, be absolutely sure that it is in writing somewhere, and that he has signed it. Again, after a dispute arises is not the time to try to remind somebody what was said months ago. Memories are too often conveniently faulty.

After you've successfully completed three or four articles for the same magazine, and they've been published without major editing jobs, you should ask for a little more money when you get offered your next assignment. If the editing or rewriting of your stuff has been heavy, you'd better wait until your writing improves a bit and this situation changes.

If you've been getting around $300 for your articles it would not be out of line to ask for 10% or even 15% more. If you've only been getting $50 or $75, even a $5 jump may be a lot for them to handle. And of course if you've been getting $600 or something like that, asking for a raise of $100 is not unreasonable at all.

When offered your next assignment, there's certainly no harm in asking nicely for more. "You haven't changed a word of my last three articles— I've shown you that I can do a really good job for you. What do you say to a little raise this time around?" To a request like that an editor would probably cautiously ask you what you have in mind—and the negotiations are on.

I have found that the very best bargaining tool is the one I just mentioned—that the editor hasn't changed a word of your articles. So if this is the case—or if he's only changed a couple of words here and there—by all means mention this. Most of the stuff that comes in to any magazine requires a lot of work on the editor's part, and he will truly value you if he doesn't have to spend much time fixing up your articles. You will really be worth more to him for this reason, and he knows that money is the best way to show his appreciation. (He also knows that once you start asking for more money you'll probably leave him soon if you don't get it. If he wants to keep you—and he will if you're good— he will even go as far as to go to bat for you with the publisher to get you a raise if he doesn't have the authority.)

Occasionally an editor will tell you that he can't make any decisions on money, and promises to speak with management "as soon as he can". If he puts you off like this more than once, you might consider not taking the next assignment until he does something. If you honestly feel that you work really hard and turn in really good stuff, and that you're being taken advantage of, you probably are. It never hurts to ask for more money. You'll probably never get it if you don't ask.

If you're really unhappy with the money you're getting and you wish to make a stand for the principal of the thing, be prepared for the possibility that your future assignments will be given to somebody else who will gladly write for the low fee. But don't let this make you afraid to stand up for yourself. If you do a really good job you will not have trouble finding other magazines that will appreciate you.

Don't forget to ask the editor about expenses when you accept an assignment. At the very least you are entitled to reimbursement for any long distance phone calls you have to make in connection with the assignment, and the magazine should also pay for any courier fees you really need. (Many magazines have accounts with couriers—be sure to ask which one they use.)

Also ask about phone calls at the time you take on the assignment. If you're in a reasonably-sized town you should be able to find plenty of people to interview locally, but ask the editor if he wants you to call some expert on the subject in New York, or some famous doctor in Houston, or Carl Sagan. If he has the budget he will probably tell you to go ahead— because it will make for a much better article. (But if he doesn't have the budget, do the best you can with the assignment by finding the best people you can locally.)

Even if the editor tells you to be free to make necessary use of long distance, always ask if there is a limit on your phone calls. I had a friend once who did a big article for a national magazine, and the editor told him to make whatever phone calls were necessary to make the article good. When the bill came in it was over $600—and the accounting department flatly refused to pay it. He could have probably taken it to court, but since that is such a hassle he settled for the $200 they offered him. The $400 he lost on the expenses was like taking a $400 cut in the payment for the article. Be sure that nothing like this ever happens to you.

In the sample contract given elsewhere in this book you'll see that there's a provision for expenses—type and limit. This contract form was written by a lawyer, and she considers it very important that you know what your limits are before you accept the assignment. Just like the other terms, you are entitled to know these things.

I have known cases of expense abuse—but these usually occur with hotel and restaurant expenses while away on assignment. When you submit your phone bill, however, you submit an actual copy of your telephone record—so it's easy for the editor to check if one of those calls was really to your Aunt Mildred in Indianapolis.

But fudging on expenses is like biting the hand that feeds you—if you're caught you'll never get an assignment from that magazine again (and probably from none of the editor's friends either). I'd hate to see a budding career end for a few bucks. It's much better to use your creative talents towards doing a better job on your assignments than towards embellishing your expense accounts—that way you'll quickly be moving up to magazines that pay better.

There is one other form of assignment you may be offered along the way, and I want to mention it here so that you will be prepared. This type of work is called "work for hire".

Doing work for hire is similar to selling all rights to something you do. It means that you write for someone else who then totally owns what you have produced.

A couple of good examples are ghostwriting and writing brochures for companies.

If someone tells you his life story, and you write it up secretly so that it looks like he wrote it himself, this is ghostwriting. There are many people—perhaps businessmen, scientists or doctors—who may need writers to ghostwrite articles for them to publish in magazines and journals, and they certainly don't want anybody to know that they didn't do the work themselves. Sometimes you'll even be sworn to secrecy.

Or if you are hired to write a brochure on dental health for a toothpaste company or for the government, they will own what you produce.

There are a couple of different ways that work for hire can be paid for. The most common is by an hourly wage. Writers can usually set their own hourly wage, and it is generally based on where you live and how much experience you have. (You can always ask for and get more in a big city.)

If you're just starting out you'll probably be able to ask around $10-15 an hour if you have some really good samples to show people—but again, it depends where you live. Writers with a lot of experience or some special expertise can easily get $50 an hour or even more in a big city. Many have a minimum per job or per day—perhaps $500.

You can generally quote your prospective client a rough amount, based on how much work there is to do and how much time you think it will take you. If there's a lot of research, for example, you may not be able to get as much money for your research time as for your actual writing time. I generally figure out my projected amount and then give people a "break" on a larger job. Doing a whole book, for example, can take forever and cost a fortune if paid for by the hour.

Remember, magazines are frequently used to paying $400 or $700 or even more for articles and do it everyday. But one businessman hiring a writer for the first time may feel that this kind of fee is far too high. (Many people feel that writing is a breeze and is not really work at all.) If he winces when you mention the fee, open negotiations. Tell him that doctors and lawyers and even plumbers all get well over $20 an hour—and you're a professional too.

Instead of an hourly fee you may be offered a set amount, and this is sometimes a good deal and sometimes not. If you do a lot of work like this, though, it will all even out in the long run. You'll lose money on some, and on some you'll make a lot more than you would have made at your hourly fee.

I mention this here so that you will be prepared if someone should ask you to do some work for hire. You should have a set fee ready for negotiation, and it should be based on how much experience you've had as a writer and on any special expertise you have. If you overprice yourself you may not get any work.

You may be able to find out the "going rate" for writers in your area by calling up some people who advertise writing services and ask them what they charge for various jobs. Joining a local writers group is helpful too—especially in setting fees and negotiating. Many groups put out a directory of members and send it around to people who hire writers. By looking in the current directory you can find out how much everybody else charges and set your fees accordingly. Many cities also have data banks which list writers and how much they charge.

Governments and other places frequently take "bids" on jobs. If you have the lowest bid, and of course are qualified, you'll get the job. I have a friend who once got over $2,000 for doing a little government health pamphlet—and she had the lowest bid! That's nice work if you can get it!

I have never tried getting work from the government, but apparently there is quite a bit of work available. You should make up a fabulous resume and put together a few fabulous samples of your work, and send this packet of goodies around to various branches of government with a covering letter asking to be put in their file of writers. (As I understand, each branch works separately and they do not communicate on matters like this—so you'll have to send out a lot of resumes.) Then when work comes up you may be hired or notified so that you can put in a bid. If you can join a writers group you should be able to find out more about this kind of work in your area of the country from them.

Whatever you do, do not neglect to get a very firm contract with anyone you do work for hire for—yes, even the government—and be sure that it spells everything out. As I said before, many individuals and companies hiring writers do so only once in a blue moon and are not familiar with the way things work. If you present yourself as a professional business-person they'll accept the terms you ask for—like when you'll get paid—without question.

For a medium-to-large job you should receive your payment in thirds—one-third in advance, one-third upon completion of half of the work, and the rest on delivery of the final work. But you will find a lot of people who will not pay you anything until everything is done—and maybe even long after everything is done. Be absolutely sure you are protected with a solid contract.

Again, always think of yourself and represent yourself as a small business. Almost everybody will accept contracts when working with businesses—that's the way things are done these days.

Unfortunately many people think that since you "only" write, and "only" work at home, you're not really working as hard as someone who works a "real" job. It will be up to you to convince them of your professionalism when you negotiate.

YOUR MANUSCRIPT

Your manuscript speaks for you—loudly. Even if an editor has met you, taken you out to lunch, etc., he still doesn't really know you until he sees what kind of work you turn in. For some of the neatest well-groomed people turn out to submit the sloppiest manuscripts, and some of the world-class slobs hand in beautiful work.

And a bad-looking manuscript turns editors off faster than anything except perhaps totally inept writing. But bad writing can be fixed. If your inner character is such that you just don't care about turning in neat work, you may never get another assignment from the recipients of your messy articles. A manuscript that is covered with purple marking pen or correction fluid has trouble even getting looked at seriously.

And that is a good part of what writing professionally is—being serious about your work. Serious. If you look neat when you meet him, and your manuscript is neat and clean too, an editor is much more willing to overlook any deficiencies in your writing. (After all, it's part of his job to fix up less-than-perfect writing. But he sure hates doing it if he can hardly read it!)

Ask any editor to give you an honest answer and he will tell you that a ridiculous percentage of the work he commissions comes in a real mess. Editors truly **value** a writer who turns in what is referred to as "clean copy". And if your copy is clean, your chances of getting another assignment from that editor skyrocket. (And don't forget that obtaining repeat work from magazines you've already appeared in is the most important work you can get. Without that you have no writing "career".)

This is also one of the reasons an editor is hesitant about trusting a new, unknown writer with an assignment. When you come to him asking for work, he may be thinking something on the order of: "Heaven only knows what kind of copy she is going to turn in, and I'm really busy next month, and don't have time to spend twenty hours cleaning up somebody's mess. I'd better go with somebody I know I can count on."

And this of course is one of the several reasons editors rely on the same group of writers, issue after issue—they have proven themselves to be totally reliable in this way. If you turn in consistently clean copy and reasonably competent writing, you're on your way to becoming a regular too!

So what exactly constitutes "clean copy"?

1. Your manuscript absolutely must be typed, and double spaced, no exceptions. If you cannot type, or cannot type well, you'll just have to get somebody to do it for you. Many editors won't even look at a manuscript that isn't typed, and I don't blame them. You may be able to read your own writing with no problem, but it's always difficult for someone else. Nobody at a magazine has the time to decipher some manuscript. And they generally won't have time to send it back to you for typing either. It will probably just be immediately rejected, and possibly even without a reading. (Yes, even if you have an assignment, your "baby" can still be rejected and never see print.)

2. It must be typed with a fresh, highly-readable black ribbon, and should be typed with Pica type or something similar. Elite can be hard on the eyes after a long day of reading manuscripts. Script typefaces and other fancy things, like all caps, are definitely out. Whatever typeface you use, be sure that it's kept spotless. Take a toothpick to your a's and o's often to make sure all the crud is cleaned out of the letters at all times.

3. If possible, use a nice even-stroking electric typewriter, but a good quality manual one is acceptable. Try to avoid some of the cheaper manuals that type only light impressions, or those which do not type perfectly straight lines. You know the kind—some letters are a little above the line, some below. Giving your editor an eyestrain tension headache is not the nicest way to start his day.

If you're lucky enough to have access to a word processor, be sure that you have a letter-quality printer. Don't ever turn in anything—manuscript or letter—in dot matrix. Many editors won't even read it—and

I was one of them when I was an editor. It's very hard on the eyes. Anything I got in dot matrix immediately went back for retyping. I stated this policy in my magazine's writer's guidelines, but many magazines will not. Don't take any chances.

Now I realize that some of the newer dot matrix printers form characters that they refer to as "near letter quality", but many editors are still prejudiced against the whole dot matrix system because of past bad experiences. As an editor, I only accepted "near letter quality" as a back-up hard copy to something that was submitted on a disk. However, your editors may not mind—but I would ask before springing a manuscript like this on them.

Severe eyestrain aside, part of the prejudice may not be in the dot matrix quality itself but in the fact that the manuscript was obviously prepared with the help of a word processor. Some editors really feel that you're not really "working hard enough" if you use a word processor to write your articles. To overcome this bias that may rightly or wrongly exist, when dealing with a new editor use a letter quality printer and do not justify your right margins—the manuscript will then look like it's been done on a very high quality electric typewriter.

After you've done a few assignments and have proven yourself perfectly capable, you might want to tell the editor that you're using a word processor. He may be thrilled to hear this news—he might be one of those who just loves to have work submitted on disks for easy editing.

4. Your manuscript must be submitted on standard size, 8½" x 11" white bond paper, no exception. No erasable bond, no onion skin, no legal size paper, no yellow or blue or purple. (And that goes for the ribbon as well as the paper.)

When I was an editor the worst manuscript I received had been typed up by one of those little lap-top computers. It was a very light dot matrix. It was on thermal paper which doesn't lie flat no matter what you do to it. And on top of that, the "writer" (I use that term loosely, because he was no professional) ripped off the manuscript into "pages" whenever he felt like it, so they were all different sizes.

If there had been time I would have returned it to him for retyping, but he was a day late as it was. No time for retyping and no time to reject it either—I had no other articles in the bank, and we'd also sold some advertising on the fact that that particular article would be in that issue. I had no choice but to struggle to type that stupid thing onto my computer. It took me four times as long as a normal manuscript—and you should have seen the headache I had when I was through!

Needless to say, that guy never got another assignment from me, and I told a couple of friends about him too. I feel that what he did was the absolute in non-professionalism.

5. There should be generous margins on each side of your manuscript pages, not just on one side. Leave at least 2″ at the top of each page, and 1½″ on all the other sides. As an added courtesy, to make room for the editor's comments and directions to the typesetter or typist, start your first page about one-third of the way down. Don't use a separate cover sheet. Just start right in on the first page, about a third of the way down.

6. Put your name, full address and phone number with area code on the first page. Then center the title of the piece. If you have no title (many editors will change what you make up anyway, and some prefer that you don't put one on), type in the subject (SPACE SHUTTLE), so that at least he knows what it is he's looking at.

If you wish, you can also enter the approximate number of words on the top right of the first page, but this is not usually necessary. He already knows how many words the article is supposed to be, because that's what he assigned—and he assumes you did what he assigned.

Many writers also type what rights they are selling on that first page. But most magazines have a policy about what rights they always buy, and your typing something different on the first page of your manuscript will not change the policy. If you did not like the magazine's position on rights, this should have been ironed out when you took the assignment.

7. On the top of every page after the first one type in a word or two from the title of your article (enough so it is easily recognized) or the subject, your last name and the page number. There are various forms; I use this style:

SPACE SHUTTLE / WEST   2-2-2-2

If you've ever seen an editor's desk you'll know why this is so very important. Things get dropped, mixed together, misplaced or simply manhandled in one way or another. Coffee gets spilled. Chances are good that something might happen to your manuscript before it's safely printed. So make it easy for everybody to put it back together again. (And always be sure to keep your carbon until the article has been safely published. One time I had to rush a carbon of the first page of a column by one-hour courier to a very frantic editor. It's a good thing I was home when he called.)

Also put a "-30-" or "end" at the end so he won't keep searching for more pages. Sometimes it's hard to tell when an article ends.

8. In spite of all the disasters that can befall your poor manuscript, mentioned above (and more), you should never staple the pages together. This is just one more courtesy—one less exasperating thing for the editor to do to get your manuscript ready for the printer. Use a paper clip if you must use something, but nothing is really necessary unless you're sending more than one manuscript at one time. In this case, do separate them for easy reading by clipping each one. Never put your manuscript into those plastic folders, weld them together with brads, etc.

9. Mail your manuscript flat if at all possible. If I have something four pages or less I will sometimes fold it in half and send it in a 5″ x 7″ envelope, but only to editors with whom I have a long-standing relationship. For all important magazines, and for the first few times you're working for anyone, send it flat. You don't have to stick a piece of cardboard in with it, but get some nice new clean envelopes and use them.

Many writers try to save money by reusing old envelopes, but I feel that this is false economy. Make your editors think they're special enough to warrant nice new envelopes. Use your old used ones to send away for catalogs and pay bills.

I've seen 10-page manuscripts stuffed into business-size envelopes, and even worse. No editor wants to receive anything that is all crunched up and/or folded to death.

It also follows that you should use the correct postage when mailing your articles in. It's a good idea to have a supply of stamps of differing denominations and a small postal scale on your desk. That will save you the trouble of running to the post office each time you want to mail something. Each magazine has its own policy of what to do with mail that comes to them "postage due"—but it makes a bad impression in any case. You're supposed to be a professional.

10. Concerning corrections: editors realize that not every good writer is a good typist. But if you're **really** bad, you should consider having your final drafts typed by someone else. The good impression this will make is well worth the money you'll pay to a typist or your kid sister.

A few corrections per page, if very neatly fixed up with white correction paper or fluid and a black pen, are acceptable. But if there are more than a few, or if you will need to blot out a whole line or something major, you'd be wise to retype that page.

A manuscript that comes in with whole lines whited out, or even worse, one that has pages that have been cut up and taped together, looks like you only did one draft, and didn't even care enough to retype it. And this leaves an extremely bad first impression. It also looks extremely bad if it's your tenth or 100th sale to that magazine. Don't ever do it.

If you show that you don't care in this way, the editor may not care to give you another assignment.

All of this dreaming and goal-setting should lead you to the moment of truth: identifying short-term financial goals that you agree are both realistic and necessary to work toward right now. The goals themselves will depend on your age and financial situation, but for most people, they're invariably practical projects that once achieved will be vital stepping-stones on the way to those more glamorous destinations.

Says Lockie: "If you happen to have lazy spending habits, gaining control over them should be a primary short-term goal. It's no use launching into a serious savings/investment program if you're loaded down with expensive consumer debt. This is where you'll need to start budgeting." Another important short-term goal: the building of an emergency cushion of cash that will cover personal and household expenses for at least three to six months. Lockie stresses that you should never count on actually using this fund—it is strictly disaster insurance.

Once you've managed to budget well enough to get the money together, stash it in something liquid but less accessible than a savings account. If the cash is ploughed into, say, savings bonds or one-year guaranteed investment certificates (GICs), you'll think twice about raiding your funds to bail yourself out at the end of an overspent month.

Once you're covered on the emergency front and reasonably clear of debt, you can start thinking seriously about those mid-range goals you identified earlier. Objectives you want to reach within the next few years, in fact, are among the most exciting goals of all. They're distant enough to be over the horizon yet just tantalizingly far enough away to keep you highly motivated.

Wealthy famous writers may be able to get away with not doing some of the things listed above, because the editor may be so anxious to get their copy that he will take it any way he can get it. But you and I cannot get away with it. Every mistake an editor finds—spelling or typing or grammar—adds up in a little book in his head. If there are just too many, or a combination of almost too many plus writing that isn't great, he may figure it's not worth the time and trouble to hire you again. And that's a fact. He has too many better things to do than to spend five hours fixing up your article—especially if he ends up doing things that you should have done yourself.

It's no excuse to say that you just can't spell. That's why they make dictionaries and spelling dictionaries. Use them. If you can't type, or don't type well, get someone else to do it for you. College students need extra money and will type for a very reasonable fee. Just make it crystal clear to the person you hire that you'll accept only so many corrections (perhaps three or four) per page, and if there are more, she will have to retype that page for you for free. And be sure to proofread everything typed by somebody else, even if she says she checked it over. Any errors an editor finds fall on your head.

If your grammar or punctuation is not perfect, get someone to check your manuscript over before you send it in. Better yet—learn your grammar and punctuation.

There is no excuse for turning in sloppy work! Sloppy work tells the editor loudly and clearly that you **don't care,** that you're not serious.

And if you don't care about him or his magazine, and are not serious about your writing career, why in the world would he give you another assignment? Or why should he even accept this one? Even if you have a contract, you know, that doesn't guarantee that your work will be accepted and published. It can always be turned down. Nothing is certain until it is actually in print.

You must realize that most of the work you will get throughout your lifetime must of necessity be **repeat work**—additional assignments from editors you've already worked for. There is a limited number of magazines that would be interested in whatever it is that you write, and soon you will have alienated them all if you prove unreliable. So you must make and keep a good solid relationship with every editor you work for. It's vital to your continuing career.

It's really true that once you've "broken into" a given magazine it's a thousand times easier to get in again—or even to become a regular contributor or contributing editor, with an article (or two or three!) in every issue. That's a wonderful position to be in, because then you don't always have to hustle for work. You know already that you've got things to do.

If you turn in perfect copy, on time, the editor will at least know that you really care, that you're really trying. Give him every opportunity to think highly of you.

I know that some of the things in this chapter may seem silly and/or picky to you. I'm sorry, but that's the way things are. Every job you might choose to do has requirements—things that you must do. And it's the same with writing. Sure, some people can get away with some things. But when you're starting out you really cannot afford to take any chances. If you really want to make a living as a writer, ignore these things at your own risk.

THE TITLE

Yes, it is true that a fabulous title will sometimes help sell a story or article. But there's an equal chance that the title will be a knock-out that the story doesn't have a chance of living up to! Every editor has waited anxiously for some assigned articles to come in, dying to read the wonderful stories to go with the wonderful proposed titles—only to be severely disappointed.

By all means suggest a title for your article. If it's especially good or unusual, you may even want to mention it in your query letter. But believe me, editors have seen so many stories that don't even begin to measure up to their titles that they're probably not going to be bowled over by yours.

If you can't think of anything good as a title for your article—and sometimes it's really hard—just write in the subject of the article. "Setting Up A Home Office" was what I put on a recent article I did for a national woman's magazine, because that was what it was about, and I honestly couldn't come up with anything spectacular. But there are a lot of very creative people on the staff of magazines, and they know their magazine's style much better than you do—so someone will come up with something. "End The Paper Chase" is what they christened my article, and I loved it! I couldn't have done half as well myself.

So don't waste a lot of time agonizing over a title. Chances are good that it will be changed anyway. Just be sure that you put something on the article, and on every page—something appropriate so the editor can tell at a glance what he's looking at.

THE SYSTEM—STEP BY STEP

You've noticed all the parts of this system all through this book. But here it is, all together now. Once you know all the guidelines, you can start fresh towards your goal of being a professional writer. Even if you've had some minor successes before, you'll do much better if you follow this system.

1. Get some professional printed stationery and business cards. (If you cannot afford both, at least get the stationery.) Even if you've never had anything published, the point is to appear—look like—you really know what is going on. Anything that marks you as an amateur sets off a warning bell in the head of any editor who has had bad experiences with amateurs before—and this is most editors. Always present yourself as a professional—and that includes dressing up whenever you visit the offices of a magazine, etc.

2. If you're not already using query letters, start immediately. Nothing brands you as an amateur faster than sending out unsolicited manuscripts. Learn to write a fabulous query letter, and make sure that it's absolutely perfect in appearance.

3. Slow and steady does it. Start out with a small, new or relatively new magazine, and do anything and everything they want. Make yourself invaluable. The experience you gain will be priceless to you.

4. Once you've learned how to handle any kind of assignment, to turn in good clean copy, to always make the deadline—and once you've had some good stuff published that you can make copies of and use as samples—start approaching larger magazines.

5. Keep approaching bigger and bigger magazines. But don't stop writing for the smaller ones until you're absolutely sure you'll be getting repeat assignments from the bigger ones. There's much more competition, relative to the number of magazines at the top. If you cannot seem to crack the

national glossies—and not everybody will be able to; there just aren't enough of them for everybody who wants to write for them—be happy working for the smaller or medium-sized magazines that appreciate you. But don't give up if you think you're good enough and can come up with appropriate ideas—keep your name in front of the biggies.

6. Never feel that you have to move up. Many people are much happier working for smaller magazines, where they feel loved and needed. Know yourself, and know what you want to accomplish in your writing career. Once you've severed a relationship with a magazine you may not be able to go back.

7. If you do want to keep moving up, keep your resume up-to-date, always reflecting the work you're getting from bigger magazines. And each time you get something really good published, or something in a big famous magazine, get good plain-paper photocopies made of that article and add it to your sample packet, replacing something from a smaller magazine.

8. Remember that the "rules" get more and more important as the caliber of the magazines you write for grows. Don't become lax. Always be dependable. Never forget that no matter how many pieces you've done for a magazine, you can always be told to take a hike. They are in charge— this is the one thing you sacrifice when you decide to be a freelancer.

HOW TO FIND NEW MAGAZINES

We are truly in a time of plenty, especially in North America. More new magazines are being started up now than at any other time in history. If you're sharp, you can hook up with a new magazine before everybody else knows about it—when there's much less competition (or none at all)—and then "grow" with it.

Some new magazines are launched with parties and great fanfare and lots of money. But I would guess that most of them are on a limited budget. Many new magazines have only enough money to put out one issue, and the backers hope and pray that it will bring in enough money in advertising and subscriptions to enable them to put out a second one. (A lot of companies will not advertise in the first issue of a new magazine; they want to see what the magazine will really look like before they commit their money to an ad.)

Also, a lot of stores will not carry a magazine until it's been out for six months or even a year. They want only a proven product. That is why it is sometimes hard to locate new magazines. Many publishers, who cannot get a contract with a professional distribution network, hire kids in Hondas to run around town leaving small piles of magazines in small variety stores on a trial basis. And unfortunately, inadequate distribution has killed more magazines than you'd ever guess—if people don't see it, they can't buy it!

However, if you keep your eyes open, and protect yourself from the worst that might happen, new magazines offer the very easiest way to break into the fabulous world of magazine writing.

Most new magazines cannot afford to pay top rates and therefore cannot expect the top professionals to want to write for them. The publishers are ecstatic if they can find competent local writers to fill their pages. What you may not get in money per article you'll certainly get in appreciation. And if you can get in at the very beginning, and can convince the editor that you can handle the work, ask to write four or five different things for each issue, under different names if he wants. In a general consumer magazine, one person can easily handle both the health and beauty columns, and also the food articles. And maybe a couple of features too.

The point I am trying to make is that even if they can only pay $50 per article, who says you can't collect several of those little checks yourself? (Always tell the editor that you've very willing to write under different names, if he wants it to look like they have more writers. Never let this stop you from getting extra work. The name really doesn't mean anything—you can still clip the article and put it in your sample packet. In the real magazine world, people write under false names all the time.)

So even if the checks are small, quantity can make up for it. And this is also very good practice and discipline. Writing four or six little articles every month is excellent training for the time when you'll move up and maybe have six big ones to do some months. When that happens, you'll have to know how to handle your time.

Of course, to get in a solid position like this with a new magazine, which will possibly grow much bigger someday (even Cosmopolitan had to start somewhere!), you must find the magazine before everybody else knows about it. When you're the first writer who comes to them, you can almost pick and choose what you want to write, and how much. And what a marvelous position to be in! "Writing your own ticket" is a great way to start your writing career.

There are five main ways to find new magazines before everybody else knows about them. If you're really fast, this can give you a good edge.

1. Read the writer's magazines for news of "new markets". This is the worst way, but if you're really good you can make it work for you. A magazine usually doesn't get printed here until after the first issue is out (or maybe even more than one issue). And just by appearing in the writer's magazine, the editor will probably get hundreds, if not thousands, of letters from people like you.

But they do need writers, and if your letter is professional-looking (printed professional stationery, perfect typing, etc.) you'll have a much better than average chance of getting noticed. If your ideas are also really good, and if you're open and flexible to whatever they want (and say so), they may consider themselves fortunate indeed that you wrote to them.

If they get hundreds of letters, only the very best will even be answered, in all probability. (The writers of letters of lesser quality may get printed form rejections in their SASEs, however.) Make sure that your letter is one of the ones that will stand out by sending along a perfect letter and good solid fresh ideas. The competition in a situation like this will be fierce—this is not the time to be slipshod. But do realize that many of the letters will be hand written, or full of errors, or just plain dumb. (When I was an editor I received many letters that stated simply: "I'd really like to write for your magazine. Can you give me something to do?")

Follow all of the suggestions in the chapters about query letters, and don't forget your SASE. Remember that most writers do not know the inside information you're learning in this book. You will have a lot of competition if you look for new magazines this way, but play it smart and you can be a winner.

2. Better than the above, but still not the best, is to constantly scout your town's largest magazine racks. And I mean at least once a week, if not more often. You should get to know them so well that you'll know by heart the position of every single magazine. In this way, if anything has been changed you'll spot it in an instant.

If you catch the first issue of a brand new magazine within a week of its first appearance on the stands, you'll probably have an excellent chance of getting in. Believe it or not, many new magazines use only a couple of writers to put together their first issue, and in some cases they're all people who are friends or relatives of the publisher. (Some very small new magazines are all written by just one person!)

If you're immediately there (in person or through your letter), and are very enthusiastic about the first issue, chances are good that the editor will greet you just as enthusiastically.

Before you get in touch with the editor, read the entire first issue from cover to cover. Study it carefully. Prepare a good and professional query letter, and get it off as soon as you can. (Remember that many other people are picking up that magazine at the same instant that you are, and you'll have to compete with them.) If it's a locally-published magazine, obviously it won't be as bad. But if it's a regional or national publication, there might be a good deal of competition. So the sooner you can get in touch with them, the better.

Your chances will be even better if the topic of the magazine is obscure or specialized. Even if you don't know much about the subject matter, you can always study up on it. Be confident of your ability to handle anything.

3. If at all possible, you should join some kind of local or national writers group or subscribe to some of the private writers' newsletters. Places like this frequently get calls from yet-to-be-published magazines when they're looking for writers. If you learn about a new magazine this way, even before the first issue is assigned, you've really discovered gold. If you can join a local writers group, they may even have a system set up whereby they call everybody when a fabulous opportunity comes along. Then you can respond immediately.

If you depend on newsletters, of course you'll have to compete with all the other people who are reading that newsletter at that moment— but the number will be limited. If you don't procrastinate—the way most of the people will—you can be one of the first to contact the magazine.

Usually the blurb will state what they are looking for, or what direction they plan to take. But even if they don't say much of anything, you can still write an acceptable query.

"I'm intrigued by the title of your magazine—I'd love to do some writing for you. Since I'm not sure which direction you plan to take, I'm certainly open to your suggestions. I can handle almost anything (and if I can't, I'll be honest and tell you). I have a special interest in the following topics: (list several, perhaps gathering some hints from the title of the magazine). If you'll kindly give me more information about the magazine, I'll rush you several specific ideas."

It's better to just say something like that than to send in a bunch of totally irrelevant and/or inappropriate ideas. Do list your areas of special interest or experience, but be sure you make it clear that you "find new challenges very exciting" and can handle whatever they want.

Send along a few tearsheets with your perfect letter, and don't forget your SASE. Even if the publisher has come out begging for writers it doesn't mean you should be less than 100% professional. In fact, the more professional your letter and package are, the better your chance of standing above the crowd.

4. If you write regularly for some magazine, the editor may tell you if the same company is planning to start up another magazine that you may be interested in writing for. Or you may be lucky enough to find out this sort of information from a neighbor or another writer. Because I belong to very active writers and editors groups and do work for so many different people I frequently hear about new magazines—and when I do I always call my friends who have an interest in that area. And then they do the same for me.

But short of inside information like this, you're on your own to scout out truly new magazines. As stated above, the absolute best deal is to find them before they've even assigned the first issue, and become one of the "founding writers". Sometimes you may even have the opportunity to help plan the magazine, and under these circumstances, it's easy to make yourself indispensable!

Magazines may hold a certain mystique to you if you haven't had a lot of experience from the inside, so you'll be surprised to know that many, if not most, small magazines are run very loosely. They may have a general plan when they start, but always need input. I have been in on the development of four magazines—I was the first writer to "find" them and they were eager to get my opinion on what they were doing. Basically, all they knew was that they wanted to start a magazine on a certain topic—and really that was about it. I suggested certain columns to them, certain areas they should cover (if I wanted to write the stuff or not), and they were incredibly grateful. It was really like they didn't have a clue as to how to go about making their magazine really complete. (Many magazines are started by people with absolutely no experience.)

Three of these were magazines for singles, and although they had planned to cover entertainment and travel, it hadn't even dawned on any of them to have food, beauty, nutrition or advice columns. I think it was because all of the principals were men—they hadn't really thought it through what women would want to read.

So I not only suggested that they include all of these things, I got to write them all too.

And this is why finding really new magazines can be such a fabulous opportunity for someone just starting out. Even if the magazine doesn't make it (and a goodly number of them will not, no matter how good they are), you will have gathered so much invaluable experience while you are helping them and writing for them.

5. So what is the best way to find these magazines while they're still in the planning stages? It's easy—you just have to read the classifieds!

Now only rarely will a magazine advertise in the want ads for writers, but it's not unknown. Keep your eyes open for this possibility, and be sure to answer the ad as soon as it appears. Ads like this usually draw the worst kinds of letters from the dumbest people who think they want to be writers. So if your letter is on printed professional stationery, and perfect, etc., you'll absolutely get a call.

If there's only a phone number in the ad, generally they will just have somebody to answer the phone and take down your number. Do not just leave your number! If you're in even a reasonably-sized town they will probably get hundreds of calls, and cannot possibly return them all. Do whatever you have to do to get the address. Tell the person answering the phone that you're a professional writer and want to send over a package of samples right away, or something like that. If you can get the address out of her, prepare your letter immediately, and even consider sending your package over by courier (don't show up in person). Couriers always impress publishers of little magazines, so you'll probably be the first person they call.

If there's an address in the ad, write the best letter you can and really make up a professional package. If it's an office address, you can send the package by courier, but you won't be able to do that if it's just a box number.

Sometimes, despite your best efforts, you will not get an answer. (It has even happened to me at the height of my career.) The only reason I can figure out is that perhaps these magazines were so small that they couldn't pay at all—or paid only a token amount. And certainly someone who had professional stationery and a resume and tearsheets and so on would not be willing to work for nothing.

But I think you will certainly turn on more people than you will turn off with a totally professional presentation. I always figured that if they didn't call me, it was their loss—and you should feel this way too. Be confident!

However, looking for ads for writers is not the main reason you should be reading the classifieds. To find truly new magazines you should be looking for the ads for the first people a magazine needs to hire—an editor, an advertising sales manager, etc.

If you take the time to really thoroughly read the want ads, in no time at all you'll see an appropriate ad. (An amazing number of magazines are being started, all over the country, all the time.)

More often than not the first ad a new publisher will place will be for an advertising salesman or manager. (They have to sell some advertising, or there won't even be a magazine—so they generally don't take on any other staff until they see how the magazine's concept is received by potential advertisers first.) So start your search of the want ads under the "Sales Agents Wanted", or whatever your newspaper calls that section of the classifieds.

You can usually skip the section entitled "Office Help Wanted", because even if they're looking for a receptionist, it probably won't say that it's for a magazine anyway. But when they're looking for an advertising salesman, they will almost always say "for new publication", or just "for publication". Selling magazine advertising is a specialized and skilled profession, and they wouldn't want to waste their time taking calls from people who are not capable of doing the job.

Also be sure to check the "General Help Wanted" and "Skilled or Technical Help" sections of the classifieds. If someone is looking for an editor they'll use one of those categories—probably the latter. If they need kids in Hondas to do some of the distribution, they'll list it in the former. Although once they're advertising for distribution people, the first issue is usually ready to roll.

If you're in a very small town you'll probably never find anything in your own local paper. So I suggest that you subscribe to just the big weekend edition of the biggest newspaper from the closest large town (or sometimes you can pick it up on Monday morning in your town's biggest bookstore). Not all magazines are started up in large cities, but if the publisher wants a top-notch editor or sales manager he will probably advertise in a paper there anyway.

If you're in a reasonably-sized town, or have easy access to newspapers from big cities, try to always read the Monday and Friday editions as well as the big weekend paper. Some people advertise only during the week, and some only on the weekends, so if you read the classifieds at least three times a week you won't miss anything. If you're close to a library, this is the best and cheapest way to check as many papers as you can. Just because an ad is from New York or Los Angeles, and you're in Peoria, it doesn't mean you can't answer it!

Once you've found an ad, then you really need all of that courage I was talking about earlier.

If there's only a phone number, you'll have to call. Ask the person who answers the phone for the name of the magazine first. After all, it may be a biggie, just in need of a new salesman. If it is, just say thank you and hang up.

If she says something that you've never heard of, just ask to speak to the editor or someone in charge. (I've even answered ads a couple of times for magazines that didn't even have names yet.) Don't ever just ask the secretary if they need any writers. She's probably been told to fend off any calls like that. And don't say that you're answering the ad for the job that was advertised either, because it may have already been filled, and they may cut you off at the pass.

If you're able to get through to anyone in charge, be straightforward and tell the guy that you love working for new magazines, that you find it challenging, and that you'd really like to send him a letter (and some samples of your work if you have any). Ask for his name and address, and if he's not too busy, see if you can find out anything about the magazine. If he says he doesn't need any writers, just say that you'd "like to drop him a note anyway, no obligation".

Many times you'll find yourself greeted with open arms. He may say that he's just started looking for writers, or that he was going to advertise for some the next week. In any case, he will admire your moxie for digging him up like this.

If he seems hesitant or unsure, tell him again that he's under no obligation, that you'd just like to drop him a note with a few article ideas, that's all—for his file. If the first issue is already assigned, tell him that you'd still like to do some work for him in the future. Say whatever you think is appropriate—whatever you have to say to just get his address. When you can write him at your leisure you can really do a good job of selling yourself.

Be sure to really read the want ads, not just skim the first words. It will be worth the time, for the best ads are usually buried in some way. The first word of an ad for an editor may be "experienced", or "needed", or even "part-time". If you only look under the word "editor" in the alphabetical listing you may miss all of them.

Also do not forget to check the "Personals" or "Business Personals" sections, as you may get some of your best leads there. Many times people are looking for partners or even collaborators, or any number of things. If you carefully read every ad you'll see what I mean. Be brave and call everybody even remotely sounding like a writer or magazine or publishing company. They won't know who you are—if it's a dead end, just say "sorry, wrong number" and hang up.

I've answered ads for "book collaborator wanted" that turned up work for me. One man in particular was working on a book, but was also planning a magazine. His project never got off the ground, but if it had, I am sure I would have been in a good position to ask for a lot of work.

Of great benefit to you in this quest for new magazines are also usually locally-published arts papers and entertainment papers. If there are none in your town, subscribe to the ones from the closest large town. Most of the "artsy" types read these—actors, artists and writers—and in many cases, if a magazine is going to advertise for writers, this is where they will do it. Also, a lot of the people who read these papers turn out to be the ones who start magazines, so you'll hear about it first if you read them (they're usually tabloids).

I still spend a couple of hours a week looking through the various papers—I truly love the challenge of writing for new magazines—and I've stumbled across all sorts of fabulous and interesting opportunities. Believe me, it is well worth the time. And if you would like to get in on the ground floor of a new magazine, you'll find that this is the easiest, and maybe at times the only way to do it. Consider the two hours or so an investment in your future.

If you have not had any luck getting assignments, even if you've been sending out perfect queries—perhaps you're simply setting your sights too high. I know you don't want to hear that. I know that you probably feel the way I used to, that you're good and that you should be able to break in at the top. That may have been possible 50 years ago, but it's seriously impossible now. There are simply too many writers. The only way you will get assignments from national magazines is to have great tearsheets to show them—and the only way you can do that is to get published somewhere else first.

I cannot stress how easy it is to get published in small new magazines. The pay may be lousy, but the tearsheets can be worth gold.

If you really (consciously or unconsciously) **like** being unpublished, so that you can have something to complain about, some reason to seek sympathy, then keep on whatever it is that you're doing. You'll succeed admirably.

But if you sincerely want to get published soon, there is no reason that you cannot. Just follow this book.

I must give you some notes of warning here about new magazines. While they are absolutely the best, and sometimes the only way to break into writing for magazines, you do have to be on your guard. Many magazines are started up by businessmen who think they'd like to be publishers. Some are started up by frustrated writers. And many are started up by people with absolutely no business experience of any kind. (Lots of people think that publishing a magazine is glamorous and will make them rich and famous.)

Now I'm not saying that any particular type of person would try to rip you off, but what I do want to say is that a high percentage of these magazines don't make it. They all start out with high hopes and expectations, but unfortunately not much money. Since there are so many new magazines being started up, competition for everything—from readers to advertising dollars—is very fierce. Only the fittest and the best-run will survive. It's imperative that you protect yourself in case the one you've hooked up with does not.

One of the best things you can do is to simply use your eyes and ears if you have a chance to visit the magazine. Do they have lavish offices, but tell you they can't afford to pay much? Too much overhead kills a lot of magazines. Does the guy promise you the earth and the stars? Many people who have nothing else to offer are the best with the talk. Don't be blinded. Keep a cool head. You may want very badly to believe that some particular magazine, which has been wonderful to you or which looks like the opportunity of your lifetime, will survive—but face the facts. Your wanting it to succeed is not enough to make it succeed, no matter how much you want it.

Use your intuition. If something just doesn't look right or feel right, you might be well-advised to pass on that one.

I told you earlier about the singles magazine that was my first big break. I ignored a lot of warning signs because I wanted things to work out so badly—it was so great being a full-time writer! Things I should have heeded? The publisher honestly felt that he was going to be the next major playboy of the western world, and even though he was deeply in debt, leased a Thunderbird and always picked up the checks wherever he went—all for effect. He also brought in a couple of expensive bottles of wine each day, and the whole staff guzzled all day long. I only went in once a week to turn in my stuff—so I don't know how bad that got. (Did I mention that the magazine folded when the publisher was convicted for conspiracy to defraud the public for the third time?)

If you choose to go ahead with a magazine you're not 100% sure of, be absolutely positive that you get something in writing for any work you're going to do. It is best to use a formal contract that spells out everything. Be sure it's signed, and that both you and the editor have copies.

If you have a contract you can use it to sue the guy in small claims court if necessary. If you have nothing, it will be hard. Even if your article has been published, and there is no cancelled check to prove that you've been paid, it's your word against the editor's what you were promised in the way of money.

But while some magazines just renege on paying writers because they don't have any money (or don't want to spend what they have on writers), some just close shop and file bankruptcy without even telling anyone. Depending on where you live, you may or may not be able to get anything from them if this happens. Generally, freelance writers are not considered "employees", and so you may be out of luck—even if you have something in writing.

Please, please do not be discouraged by any of the above. Most new magazines will pay you without any trouble, even if they decide not to put out a second or third issue. Most of them start out with just enough money to finance the first couple of issues, and they will know by then if they will be able to continue. If the magazine gets no subscribers and the salespeople have great difficulty selling ads, any smart businessman will admit he had a bad idea and move on to something else. It is only the unscrupulous few who will try to keep going when the money runs out.

I have been ripped off by a few new publications, but in my view, I still think it's worth taking the chance. You can deduct the "bad debts" from your income tax and that will be the end of it. (One good thing about writing for small new magazines that don't pay much is that even if you do get ripped off, you won't lose much!)

Getting into a new magazine may be your only route to being published. And if you cannot make those first few sales, you'll never be able to move on to bigger and better things. So even if you gamble and lose with your first publication or three, you'll still have tearsheets to show to other magazines. And that is relatively the only way to move up.

So protect yourself as well as you can, but don't be paranoid about it. Also be careful about letting the editor or publisher know if you're unsure of his chances for success. If you're highly enthusiastic about the magazine—whatever it is—they'll want you around, and will be fair with you even if things don't work out. (And who knows, they may use the experience they've gathered to start another magazine that will succeed— and you can be a part of that.)

If you do happen to get ripped off, consider it a learning experience and move on. So you've invested ten hours in doing an article for which you got no pay in the end. You probably would have spent that time writing anyway on your own, but the article wouldn't have been published. Grab a half-dozen copies of the issue your article is in and run. All you need are those tearsheets.

I want to warn you here about one other thing that a magazine may try to pull on you. It's usually a new magazine that will do this, and some may do it by necessity. But some magazines, even if they're twenty years old and well-established, are still struggling, just like some new magazines are. So the editor may tell you that he can't pay you for your article until three months after it's been published. (He will probably say something like: "As soon as the advertisers pay us, we'll pay you".) Now that is okay in itself, because advertisers frequently don't pay until months after they're supposed to—and this is where most magazines get most of their funds. And it is indeed the case that some magazines work so close to the wire that they honestly cannot scrape up an extra $20 without a lot of warning.

First, make sure that every writer is getting the same treatment and the same story. If you're the only one being asked to wait, beware! And second, be absolutely sure that you have everything in writing, including the approximate date you can expect payment for your work. And third, you have to be firm about how far you will let this go.

One of the magazines I used to do a lot of writing for, a bi-monthly, was always short on money. I always had to wait an inordinate amount of time. I stupidly did the first two issues (about 3-4 articles per issue) before I got a cent, and it really added up—by that time he owed me well over $1500. It was at that point that I put my foot down. I refused to do any more work until I got everything that was owed to me.

The scenario went like this, and was repeated exactly like this every single time: He would call and say he had chosen what he wanted me to do for the next issue from my list of ideas. I would say fine, I'm anxious to get started, and I will the minute I get my money from the last issue.

He would call a couple of weeks later and ask how the articles were coming, and I'd tell him I haven't even started yet because I haven't gotten the check. Since the deadline was fast approaching, he would usually send it then—but sometimes there was a third or fourth phone call before it sunk in that I meant business.

By working like this, even if the magazine had bit the dust while I was writing for it and I was left unpaid, I would have only been unpaid from one issue. It was still a reasonable amount of money—but it would have been an awfully lot worse if he had owed me from two or even three issues.

I remained inflexible about this, and he always managed somehow to scrounge up the money and send it to me just in time for me to complete the stuff for the next issue. Some of the other writers, who did not insist on this pay-as-you-go system are for all I know still waiting for money from several issues ago. But he wanted me to write for him, as I wrote very good stuff and had never let him down, and he always managed to find the money for me.

I recommend that you follow this plan also. Don't let them take advantage of you. Remember that you are the owner of your own small business, and you have every right to be treated like any businessperson. If they tried to pull something like that on the printer, he would tell them to go jump. You should too. Stand up for your rights. Sooner or later it usually sinks into the head of even the hardest-headed publisher that without writers he doesn't have a magazine. It is then that he usually cleans up his act. By standing up for yourself, you will hasten the day that this happens for yourself and all the other writers.

GOOD ANSWERS TO GOOD QUESTIONS

These are some of the questions that have been received from readers since the first edition of this book came out.

The biggest problem I seem to have is with getting ideas. When I do come up with a good idea I have no trouble selling it—but getting the ideas is like pulling teeth. Do you have a secret that you can share?

Believe it or not, I used to have this same problem. I used to find it very difficult to come up with good ideas, but over the years I have been able to train myself to find them anyway. Remember that magazines do not want you, per se, they want your ideas. Finding writers is easy—but magazines need to find writers with good ideas. And this is **not** always easy. Your chances of a very successful career really depend as much on your being able to come up with lots of good ideas as being a good writer.

Start by getting several little pads of paper and pens and put them all over the house—especially by the TV, the telephone and the bed. If you start to pay attention to your daydreams and reveries you'll soon notice that you do gets wisps of ideas. But they generally disappear as fast as they come to you, so you'll have to capture them immediately. With paper and pens everywhere, one will always be handy. Jot down even two or three words—just enough so that you will be able to recall what it was you thought of.

Then when you have time, gather your pieces of paper and see if there's anything of value there. Sometimes there will be, and sometimes there won't. But you'll find yourself getting better at this as time goes by.

My most fruitful idea-seeking times, however, have been when I was looking through old magazines.

When I got my first assignment from one particular big national glossy I really wanted to do a great job, so I gathered together the last 15 or so issues of that magazine and went through them page-by-page. (I had been saving them because I knew I'd be writing for this magazine one day—but you could do the same thing at a library.)

I had a pad of paper next to me because I had planned to make notes on how other people did their articles, but I ended up filling two whole sheets of paper with ideas I got while reading each issue. I still have the 30-some pages I wrote during that session, and I have so many good ideas on those sheets that they'll keep me busy for a long time. I sent many of the ideas to that magazine, but many I've sent elsewhere.

If you try going through some old issues—of almost any magazine— you'll see what I mean. Just let your mind wander. For example, they may have run a big article on old-fashioned picnics. By free associating you'll come up with all kinds of ideas for articles—ideas on those new catered champagne picnics, romantic picnics for lovers, new designs in picnic baskets, new designs in thermos containers, how to start a barbecue easily, unusual meats for barbecuing, preventing food poisoning, new advances in frisbee playing (a favorite picnic pastime), teaching dogs to play frisbee, and on and on.

Once you train yourself to start free associating, you'll find that you do it constantly—especially during TV shows. Just be sure to write everything down, or you'll forget.

You may want to start an ideas notebook to gather together all of these fabulous ideas—or perhaps a card file. A good idea will never be wasted—you'll usually be able to find somebody to sell it to eventually. Almost everything has a market.

When you start sending out your two or three query letters a week, each containing three or four article suggestions, you'll need a lot of ideas. Go to the library and read through all kinds of magazines for the last couple of years. You'll be amazed at how many ideas you get, and how quickly you find the cure for your problem.

I would like to start building a really good reference library to assist me while I write. Can you tell me which books you use the most, and which ones I would find useful?

I have bought most of the interesting books that have come out about writing over the years, but most of them I just read once and discard. The really valuable books, the ones I use all the time, are right in front of me on my desk.

I have the small paperback *Merriam-Webster Dictionary* right next to my computer, and use this all the time to check spellings. But on the desk I have the *Webster's New Collegiate Dictionary,* which I use to look up the occasional word that isn't in the little one, or when I am trying to choose a word and need to see complete definitions. But the big one would be a pain to use for just quick spelling checks.

The books I use next most often are the thesauri—I have three, and occasionally do need them all. I recommend that you have more than one, simply because some perfect words are hard to put your finger on, and it's easier with three different methods of location. If I get frustrated with one, I just grab another.

I also frequently use a book called the *Dictionary of Problem Words and Expressions* (Harry Shaw, McGraw-Hill, 1975). I've also recently obtained a big book called the *Harper Dictionary of Contemporary Usage* (William and Mary Morris, Harper & Row, 1985), and it is excellent. Both of these books explain the subtle and not-so-subtle differences among words and usages, and help me make sure that I don't make mistakes in this area.

Of course you'll want to have the most recent copies of the *Writer's Market* and *The Writer's Handbook.* And if you write fiction or poetry or songs, Writer's Digest Books also publishes market books for you. These books change quite a bit each year, so you should always have the most recent copy. There's also an interesting book called *The International Directory of Little Magazines and Small Presses,* which is published yearly by Dustbooks. This book contains thousands of listings that are not in the other market books, and is particularly useful if you write poetry or what is called alternative literature.

You'll also want a good grammar reference book, but I hate to recommend one—since I have never yet found one that I really love. I find them all a little difficult to use, and usually have to spend far too much time looking something up. The skinny ones that are easier to use never seem to have the fine points that I need—or maybe I just can't find them. But I have six of these books, and sometimes I need all of them to find something.

The last book I can recommend most highly, which you'll need only if you use a word processor or are into editing or book publishing, is the *New Webster's Word Divider.* Word processors and computerized typesetting equipment have one great fault—they frequently do a lousy job of hyphenating. So if you're editing, you'll have to check almost every computer-generated hyphen. This little book is great for that, and there's only the rare word that I need that isn't in there.

With a basic library like this, you should be prepared for almost anything.

I have come up with some good ideas that the editors I've sent them seem to like, but for some reason they don't want me to write the articles. I've had about a dozen articles published, but it was hard getting those assignments—I almost had to talk the editors into giving me a chance. Maybe I'm not good enough. But in any case, I've been giving away some ideas to editors who really seem to want them—figuring that by being accommodating about this maybe they'll give me some assignments eventually—but then I kick myself every time I see one of "my" articles written by someone else. What should I be doing?

Well, you should certainly stop giving away your ideas. Coming up with good ideas is frequently much harder than writing, and if you have the "gift" of getting them you should guard them with your life.

However, it does indeed happen (and more often than a lot of beginners realize) that editors want only a writer's ideas—and not the writer. Perhaps they have enough good writers and don't want to take the time to break somebody new in, or like you suspect may be your case, they may feel that you're not experienced enough to handle the great assignments that come with your great ideas.

What should you do the next time this comes up? You definitely deserve something for coming up with the ideas, and you should put a price on them. It is generally considered fair that the originator of the idea should get ten percent of the fee that the person who writes the article will be getting—and then the writer gets the other 90 percent.

No editor should quarrel with this, because he is not paying out any extra money, but he may protest that the writer will complain about only getting 90 percent of his or her regular salary. But if I were you, I would hold my ground. If he refuses to pay you this ten percent, then inform him that you will take your ideas elsewhere. (You have this right.)

But chances are good that if he likes this idea he will want to get others from you—even if he doesn't want you to write them up. People with good ideas are very valuable to an editor.

So do stand up for yourself. If you've given this particular editor a freebie before, tell him that that one was a gift but that you expect to be paid for any more he may want in the future. If it's a new editor who asks for an idea, tell him it's your policy to charge ten percent of the fee for the idea. Ask what the writer would normally get for doing that article, and just figure out your share.

Once an editor agrees to this kind of arrangement, be absolutely sure that you get something in writing—the amount you will be paid and when you'll get it (and you should probably also ask about kill fees, in case the writer he chooses does a lousy job with your idea). If he won't give you a letter or sign a contract (you can adapt the contract given in this book to fit this situation), then you should send him a letter covering all of the facts, and stating that if you don't hear from him in 7-10 days (put in the exact date and year) you'll assume this information is correct. Keep a copy. Then just send him an invoice.

Never be afraid to stand up for your rights and to ask for what should fairly be yours. It may not seem like it, but editors do truly respect writers who stand up for themselves. Those who took your ideas before probably do not respect you because you were so easy to take advantage of—and you probably won't get any work from them.

I come up with some good ideas for articles, but have never gotten an assignment because I am afraid to send these ideas to editors—I'm afraid my ideas will be stolen. Does this happen often?

I have heard a few stories of this happening, and used to think that I even had some evidence. Three people, all of whom I knew well and trusted, told me that one particular big local magazine had taken their ideas; they all said that the printed articles were exactly what they had suggested. However, I began to seriously wonder about this sort of thing once I became an editor.

The magazine I edited was tiny compared to most others, but I received probably about 100 ideas in the ten months I edited it. So I would imagine that big magazines get thousands of ideas every year.

And just as most of the ideas I got were exactly the same—so must the ideas being sent in to other magazines.

All humans have a collective history and memory, and I feel that we all truly do come up with many of the same ideas at the same time. When I listed some ideas I came up with upon reading that picnic article (see the first question, above), I'm sure those were the same ideas you would have come up with after free associating about picnics for a while. And while your approach may have been slightly different—perhaps you'd want to do a picture spread of thermos bottles shaped like cartoon characters, and I might have wanted to do an article on how they come up with and test market new thermos designs—we still basically had the same idea.

So if I had my idea rejected, and then saw your article in the magazine three months later—I might have felt that they "borrowed" my idea. But in reality, you just thought about picnics at the same time I did, and sent these various ideas to the same magazine at about the same time, and they liked your approach better than mine. They may have, in fact, had twenty different thermos ideas to choose from when they had their story meeting—or maybe even fifty.

I now feel that ideas occasionally may have been stolen many years ago, but I seriously doubt that it happens these days. There are too many good writers submitting great ideas—I'm sure editors have no shortage of ideas. I'm also sure that editors look at so many thousands of ideas all the time that none of them really stick in their minds—unless they really want them. And if they want your idea, they'll probably call you to develop it rather than "borrowing" it and giving it to somebody else. I believe that there's enough honor in the profession.

Of course, there have also been legal actions taken against a few editors who have been accused of stealing ideas—and if for no other reason, I'm sure editors stay away from this sort of thing simply because writers are watching them so closely.

You should never be afraid to send out your ideas—you must have the courage to plunge right in and ask for assignments. It's the writers who ask for it that get all the work. If you want to write, sooner or later you will have to send out some ideas. If you're too afraid to send them out because you feel they may be stolen, then maybe that isn't really the problem. Maybe you're just too afraid of rejection, and are using this as an excuse or smoke screen. Think about this possibility.

I frequently get great assignments, but always have a lot of trouble finding really good people to interview. I know my articles would be better if I could find better experts. What do you suggest?

You've raised a good question here. I've generally found that there is always one single person who really "makes" every article. Having the good fortune to quickly and easily find this most perfect person to interview can cut the time you spend on an article in half.

I know that sometimes this is impossible—and sometimes you have to make seventy calls before you even get a lead. But I have discovered a few shortcuts along the way, and maybe you will find them helpful.

It took me a while to learn about this, but most places like universities, hospitals, police and government departments have public relations people—liaison officers, if you will. Whenever you need someone at a big place like this, ask the switchboard operator about it. Once you can talk with this special liaison person, explain in detail what your article is about. He or she is supposed to know everyone on the staff and what they do, and should be able to recommend the best person for you to speak with—but can only do this if you give sufficient data. If you give incomplete or misleading information you may be given the names of all inappropriate experts.

Generally you leave your request, and either the liaison person will get back to you the next day or so with a few possibilities or your name and number will be given to the potential interviewees and they will call you directly. This can frequently take a week (or even more)—so allow yourself plenty of time.

Once you've gotten the names of some supposedly-perfect people, talk to them (or at least their secretaries) for a few minutes before you arrange an appointment if you can. Just very briefly outline what you're planning to ask them during the interview, and see what kind of reaction you get. This is really important, since often even the most highly touted expert will just not be the right person for the needs of your particular article, and he may quickly recommend someone else to you who will be better. You don't want to waste time on appointments that won't pan out.

This is especially important with lawyers, doctors and the like. People are so specialized these days that the doctor who could make your article on diseases of the right kidney may not be able to help you at all with your article on left kidneys. (This is exaggerated, of course—but you know what I mean.) You could easily end up making a hundred appointments, each of which only lasts four minutes as you're referred to somebody else.

If the people you need to find are not associated with some big organization that may have a liaison person, then you're on your own. Here are some tips:

If it's doctors, lawyers, dentists, veterinarians, architects, even accountants, etc. that you need, you'll find that these people all have professional associations. You may have to call your nearest large town to find them—but they should be able to help you. Tell them you need experts on left kidneys, or divorce, or art deco, or tax shelters, or whatever, and ask them to recommend somebody close to you (if you don't have free reign with long distance expenses). The referred people may not be the right ones you need, but they know most of their colleagues and will generally be able to pass along the names of other people who will be better suited to your article if they can't help.

You should also start a special card file with the names of people who have been very helpful to you in the past. Maybe they couldn't answer your questions themselves, but were always anxious to help you find somebody who could help. They'll be glad to help again. Also keep people that you have already interviewed in your file—once they see their names in print they're always more than happy to talk with you again. And they will always remember who you are.

If you need a very special doctor, lawyer, public health official, or whatever—call one of these people who've helped you in the past, tell your story, and ask for exactly what you need. Chances are good that you'll get a few good leads. And if none of them pan out, you'll get further leads from these new people. This may seem like a long process, but believe me, it's much better than starting cold with a phone book.

You should also start an article file. I've been doing mine for years, and now it fills five full drawers of a file cabinet. I have file folders for everything I am interested in, and in great detail. Since I write a lot on medical topics, for example, I have separate folders for each organ, each common disease, each item of concern, etc. I save absolutely anything and everything I can find on these subjects. (And that's why my files now fill five drawers.) When I want to do an article on the mind-body connection in arthritis, for example, I check all of the old clippings in the arthritis file and the mind-body file. Frequently I find the most perfect person to interview in one of these other articles. (Although to actually **find** him I may have to call the magazine that originally printed the article, leave a message for the writer if she's not on staff, and wait for her to get back to me.)

Of course local clippings dealing with local people can be more valuable since these are the people you'll be interviewing the most. To put together a good file on local people, read every newspaper and local magazine in your city and clip everything of interest. It takes a while to set up and maintain a file like this, but it is really valuable—both for finding people and for finding ideas. (Once an editor called me and said that he needed an article on hair for the next issue. I grabbed my "Hair" file and started throwing ideas at him until he heard something he liked. Old article are priceless for piquing ideas.)

Your city may also print all kinds of little directories—health services directories, shops and services, lists of government departments, etc. Be sure to buy them all and save them. They can really come in handy.

If you can join a local writers group, you'll also find this invaluable. I have had occasions when I couldn't find anyone good to interview, and have taken my writers group directory and searched until I found some people who specialized in the needed area. I called them, and have usually been able to get several good leads from their personal files. (Most professional writers do have extensive files—that's why I recommend that you start yours now.)

If you feel that you're not finding the best people to interview, then maybe you simply need to spend a little more time at it. There are always great people out there—and you will find them eventually. Just make another couple of calls. If you don't have enough time, then perhaps you've waited until the deadline got too close before you started. Always allow enough time to find the people and do the interviews. Even if you don't want to actually write the article until the night before it's due because you work best under pressure—at least start looking for the people you'll want to interview as soon as you get the assignment. An editor can tell if the whole assignment has been put together in three days—because the people interviewed will usually be way below average. Great people can be found—just allow yourself enough time.

I frequently spend days or weeks on short articles and sometimes can do a big article in just a couple of days. I've never had anything rejected, and my editors have in fact told me that I do really good work. I never know how much time to spend on an article, and sometimes feel like I've wasted a lot of time for low pay. Any suggestions?

What happens to you happens to all writers all the time. If there is an article that is particularly dear to your heart, or one that you know a lot about, you can usually do it in no time at all. I've done some big articles in one draft completely from facts in my head—I didn't even have to look anything up, let alone call anybody for information. And then I've had little articles that took weeks, either because I didn't have a clue how to do them or else didn't really want to do them.

But don't be dismayed. It all averages out in the end. The rare article that you can write from your head may earn you $300 an hour—but you'll have some that earn you only $5 an hour.

If you are always having trouble and taking what you feel is an inordinantly long time to do your stuff, maybe you're trying to tackle articles that you have no interest in or that you simply find very difficult. Try thinking through your ideas better before you send them out. Think about exactly what you'll have to do to execute those ideas if you should get the assignment. If you are sending out complicated ideas that would require you to find and interview 36 nuclear physicists, attend 20 foreign operas, or read 17 books on philosophy, then you can't complain when the article takes you a long time to do.

Try coming up with ideas about things you have more knowledge about, or things that you'd like to learn more about. Then it will be a pleasure to do the articles, and you won't feel like you've toiled for too many hours.

I don't seem to have too much trouble getting the occasional $1000 article assignment—but then I worry so much about doing a good enough job that I spend 40 hours a week for over a month solid to do the article. I know I'm spending too much time, and that my "hourly wage" for this sort of article works out to be pretty low. But I feel a great responsibility and pressure when I am offered such a high-paying assignment, and keep doing more interviews and research and keep rewriting a hundred times. I've always gotten praise for these articles—but they take a lot out of me. I think I'd do even a better job if I could relax—how can I learn to relax in this situation?

It's wonderful to have assignments for $1000 articles, and you can be very proud of yourself that you can get them—not everybody can. But you're right—the time spent on a complicated massive $1000 article can frequently be much more than that required to do ten $100 articles, which can sometimes be done very quickly.

If you want the satisfaction or the prestige that comes with having articles in big important magazines, you must realize that they always take a lot more time to research and write. This is the price you pay.

If your main concern is money, rather than the prestige or fame you get by being in big magazines, you can make just as much money in a lot less time by only going after quantities of lower-paying assignments. Or, putting it the other way—if you like working 160 hours a month you can make a lot more money by seeking out and taking lots of little articles that won't take much more than two or three hours each to do. In 160 hours of solid work you should be able to do over fifty $50 or $100—or even $200—articles. That adds up to a lot more than $1000.

Of course, finding fifty little assignments like that to do month after month can take a lot of time and effort, but it can be done. Rather than always looking for new work and new markets, make it easy by hooking up with ten or twenty (or more) little magazines that really appreciate your work, and do more than one thing for each of them—in a big city this would not be difficult. It may take a little time to find all of these markets, but once your network of little magazines is all set up you'll never have to look for work again. Ever.

This is basically the way I worked. I much preferred doing lots of little articles, and only had one assignment that paid over $1000 in my whole career, although I had quite a few in the $700-800 range. I found doing a lot of constantly-changing little things much more interesting than spending dozens of hours on one thing.

You should have a talk with yourself and decide exactly where you want to go with your writing career. If you want to become a well-known writer, then it looks like you're well on your way. But if the stress is going to kill you before you're 40, then that's another story. Decide what is really important to you—having prestige and fame, having more money, more leisure, more time for your family, making your living with the least amount of stress, whatever—and then change things so that you get it. If you're getting these great assignments you're obviously very talented—you can do whatever you want. All you have to do is decide what is really the most important thing to you and then go for it.

I've written a book that I know would sell well in my local area. I'm also quite well-known through a weekly column I write, and I know many of my readers would buy the book. I'd like to publish it myself so that I can keep all the profits instead of sharing them with a publisher, but I haven't got a clue how to get started. Please give me any suggestions you have.

There's a lot you'll have to learn, but fortunately none of it is difficult at all—in fact, it will probably be the most interesting thing you've done in a long time. There are several excellent books out that will show you everything you need to know, in an easy step-by-step manner. The most thorough are *The Complete Guide to Self-Publishing* by Marilyn and Tom Ross, available through Writer's Digest Books, and *The Self-Publishing Manual* by Dan Poynter, available from Para Publishing, Box 4232-P, Santa Barbara, CA 93103-0232. Although much of the information in these books is the same, there are some things in one that are not in the other, so you'll probably want both of them.

You should also really join the American Bookdealer's Exchange, which has a wonderful magazine packed with invaluable marketing and promotional tips as well as all kinds of resources and special help (all of the members are small publishers who believe in helping each other). They also offer a complete consultation service and many other benefits. For further information, please drop a long SASE to Wealth Unlimited, Box 256-N, Station Z, Toronto, ON M5N 2Z4 Canada. (They also have a great catalog of books on self-publishing—just ask for one when you write.)

You will learn from all of these resources one important fact—that writing your book is only about 30% of the work. The other part is the marketing and promotion. Because if nobody knows about your book, nobody will be able to buy it. Fortunately there are also several excellent guides out about promoting and marketing your books (some are available through Winslow Publishing—see the order form on the last page of this book).

I'm sure you'll sell a lot of books through your column, but if you really want to be successful and make a lot of money, that probably won't be enough. You'll need to learn to prepare a really great press kit and use it properly to get yourself some free publicity in other people's columns and other places. You will probably also want to do some advertising.

Many book stores will not carry books from independent presses, so you may find, like many others have, that a successful mail order campaign is the secret to making a lot of money with your product.

It seems to be nearly impossible for the average good writer to get a book published by a big publishing house these days. It is my understanding in fact that only about ten percent of the books written each year get published, and I think that's a real shame. Even if you can get a big publisher interested in your book, it seems like many of them only spend their promotional dollars on the well-known writers and the big blockbusters, leaving the mid-list to languish on the shelves virtually unknown and unsold. Because of this I believe that small independent publishers will take up the slack, so to speak, and begin to offer some of the most interesting books around. There's no reason why you cannot be successful in this area. It will take a reasonable amount of work, but I think you'll really enjoy putting together a book and seeing the results of your hard work really pay off. If you have a good product—and by that I mean a book of relatively universal appeal and interest—you can make some very good money indeed.

If you'd like a free booklet explaining how the publisher of this book started her successful small press and how you can do the same, please send three loose stamps (American or Canadian) to Carolyn Winslow, Winslow Publishing, Box 413-N, Station Z, Toronto, ON M5N 2Z5 Canada. Please request *An Introduction To Self-Publishing With Resource List.*

I've been having no trouble getting assignments—people always seem impressed with me and my tearsheets—but more than half of the articles I do are rejected. I have to always keep looking for new places to hire me, and that's a pain. What are the main reasons for rejection of articles, and what can I do to improve my batting average?

There are several reasons for rejection, but I feel that the most important of these is simply an inadequate job on the content of the article.

Although editors don't **like** messy manuscripts, lots of spelling and grammar mistakes and less-than-great writing, it is, after all, their job to fix up this kind of stuff. Articles will not generally be rejected just because they're a mess. (You may never get another assignment from that magazine, but they'll generally accept this one, even though messy, if the content of the article is good.) And that's the point—they will be much more liable to accept a manuscript like this if the article itself is good. If the article looks like a mess and is **also** inadequately done, chances are excellent for rejection.

But even if the writer submits perfect copy the article can still be garbage. Some writers don't like doing research or interviews and try to do articles from their heads when they know little or nothing about the subject. I've seen articles that did not have one interesting fact or one important observation—they were just nothing at all. I've also seen articles that were full of nothing but the writer's own supposed facts and personal observations, most of which were faulty or ridiculous.

Magazines simply cannot afford to print articles like that. The continuing success of a magazine depends primarily on the money that comes in through subscriptions and advertisements—and if the magazine prints garbage, nobody will want to read it or advertise in it.

If you've been accepting rejection without asking why, you should start asking now. Once you know exactly what the problem is you should be able to fix it. But I suspect that you're simply not doing a good enough job with the content, the meat, of the articles.

Try spending more time finding good people to interview—or start interviewing several people if you haven't been doing this—and ask them interesting and thorough questions. Do whatever research is necessary to adequately cover the topic. Maybe you should ask someone to read over your next article before you send it in. Tell him what the article is supposed to be about, and then ask him if there's anything else he'd like to know about the subject after he's read it. If he comes up with a dozen different points or unanswered questions, you probably could do a lot more work on your article before you consider it finished. (If the articles you're trying to do are so complicated that you really have trouble getting the meat, then why not try submitting ideas that would be easier for you to handle?)

Do the best job you can and be sure to type up your manuscript perfectly, and everything should be okay. It sounds like you just probably need to spend a little more time working on your assignments.

A 3,000-word article I've written has been accepted for publication by a trade magazine. The editor told me that I'll be paid between 5-25 cents a word for it when it's published, but I don't know when that will be. The last letter I got from him was about six weeks ago. I was afraid to be too pushy about a contract—what should I do? I don't want to blow my chances of this article getting published.

This is a good example of why writers try to get magazines to agree to payment on acceptance. This magazine of yours is holding all the cards, and you've let it happen by not insisting on a contract. Technically, the magazine could hold on to your article for months, and then they may never publish it. And since you agreed to payment on publication, you'd never get paid. If you make a fuss, they have the right to just return the article to you and say "sorry".

What can you do now? In any cases of dispute with a magazine, I much prefer to write letters than to call—you might get the editor at a bad time. I'd write him a nice friendly letter (date it and keep a copy) asking when he intends to publish your article (name it). If there is no response, wait ten days or two weeks and write again. Keep writing every two weeks until there's a reply. If there is no reply after five or six letters, I would think you're entitled to say that you'll go over his head (mention the publisher of the magazine by name, like you know him), if this last letter isn't answered. If it isn't then drop a note to the publisher. This is occasionally necessary. (Some publishers never visit their magazine's offices and depend on the editor to keep them informed on what is going on. But as you know, some editors really do lousy jobs, and you'll be helping all of the writers if you let the publisher know.) Just explain to him that the editor will not answer your letters, and you'd like to know the status of your article.

You may not want to take this action because you figure it will kill your chances of ever getting into that magazine—and it might. However, magazines that don't answer letters and/or return phone calls also frequently don't pay writers—and you're probably better off to say "good riddance to bad rubbish" and try to sell your article elsewhere. (Very few articles are so specialized that they can't be sold somewhere else with minor adjustments.)

You must, however, inform the editor in writing that you are withdrawing your article from his consideration before you try to sell it elsewhere—and I'd do this by registered mail.

Now let's get back to why you got into this mess in the first place. There are some magazines that are in serious financial trouble, and then there are some that are simply run by unethical people who will take advantage of writers at any opportunity. They figure that nobody will sue for just a couple hundred bucks, and they're probably right.

You absolutely must protect yourself. I cannot stress this strongly enough. I recommend that you never do anything else without a contract, and be sure that it spells out not only how much you will be paid but also the date you will be paid. If an editor is adamantly against putting something in writing about your assignment you should be very wary—because there's a reason why he doesn't want to.

The time has come now when everybody in business is using contracts, and you must also. Most editors will welcome contracts and be impressed by your business-like approach to your assignment by asking for one. If you get nothing but flack from some magazines, I would seriously think twice about accepting those assignments.

Nobody is going to protect you from getting taken advantage of except yourself. It sounds like this episode was a good learning experience—I hope it gives you the courage to stand up for your rights in the future.

Some months ago I wrote an article and sent it unsolicited to a local newspaper, and they printed it one Saturday. I didn't hear back and never got a check, so I phoned the editor. He told me to not be silly, that newspapers don't pay for articles. Is this true?

I hate to say this, but you were ripped off. While it is true that some small newspapers don't pay some freelancers—they try to get as much stuff as they possibly can for free—the editor should have told you this before he printed your article.

But unfortunately there is nothing you can do now. Chalk this one up to experience, and use copies of that article as samples of your work when you look for some better places to write for!

I cannot say this often enough—you simply must get something in writing when you work for someone. If you had done this, you would have found out up front that this newspaper didn't pay—or if you had asked for some money ahead of time you might have gotten some.

You sent this article out as an unsolicited manuscript, and I suppose that some small out-of-the-mainstream publications may still feel that if somebody sends them something they are free to use it for free. People are always sending things, especially to local papers, and they never expect payment. This is why so many editors feel that they don't have to pay for anything sent in to them unsolicited.

If you put yourself forward as a professional writer, by sending out a query first with samples of your work, you'll be treated as a professional, and will be paid for any assignments you're given. And if the magazine cannot pay, at least they'll tell you at the time you're offered the assignment—then it's up to you to decide if you want to work for nothing but the tearsheets.

Don't forget, you have the right to ask how much money you'll be getting and to negotiate with the editor if the amount is unacceptable. If you never ask, or if you send out unsolicited manuscripts to places like this, you can't get too upset if you don't get paid. A big newspaper or medium-to-big magazine should not pull something like this on you— but with small local publications, you have to keep in mind that things like this can and will happen. Protect yourself.

I recently got a letter from an editor suggesting the "slant and focus" he wanted for an article I was writing on spec. He seemed to use these terms interchangeably, but I feel that's wrong. Could you explain the difference?

You're lucky that you got something in writing from that editor. We writers absolutely love magazines that send out assignment letters—they're so helpful. I've always felt that editors who don't take the time to prepare assignment letters deserve it when they get stuff that needs a lot of editing.

Slant and focus are similar but not exactly the same. Focus is exactly what it sounds like. If you're doing an article on a local politician, for example, you can focus on his campaign promises, his personal life, his views on abortion, why he spent time in jail last year, etc. Any subject has a thousand different aspects you can focus on. It's an excellent idea to ask the editor what he wants you to focus on before you start an assignment, because you might choose the wrong or inappropriate thing altogether and then have to rewrite.

Slant is more the way you look at the thing (the aspect) you've chosen to focus on. If your editor wants the article to be about why the politician is pro-abortion, for example, you can slant that article to make the guy sound like either a humanitarian or a murderer. Slant obviously only comes into play when you're writing about something that has options. If you're doing an article on something like the opening of a new jewelry store, there's not much call for slant (unless of course you feel that there are already too many jewelry stores and that jewelry stores are a blight on the neighborhood).

If you're unsure of what the editor wants—ask. If you don't ask, and do the wrong thing, you have no one to blame but yourself if you have to take the time to rewrite.

I always just barely make the deadlines for my articles. No matter when I start I'm still up typing until dawn the night before everything is due.

I guess I need to learn to manage my writing time better. What works for you?

Believe me, I still have the occasional time when I am up typing until dawn too—sometimes it can't be helped. Sometimes that one person you really must interview is out of the country until the day before your article is due. But to put yourself through this stress every time you write an article will burn you out very quickly.

Most writers procrastinate at one time or another—and some do it all the time. Many feel that they can only do good work under pressure, if the deadline is breathing down their neck. Other times it is simply that the assignment is difficult or something they don't have the slightest bit of desire to do.

But the editors must have the articles on time—the deadlines wait for no one. So whatever your excuse for not starting on your articles sooner, you really should try to overcome it.

I find that even if I don't want to actually write the article right away when it's assigned, which may be two or three months before it's due, at least I start doing the research and interviews. If you're not sure enough of your note-taking, (I mean not sure that you'll be able to get enough down to remember what was said if you do the writing a month or more after the interview), then start taping all of your interviews. You'll end up spending more total time this way because you'll have to listen to the tapes again right before you do your writing, but this may solve your problem anyway.

I'm the kind of writer who likes to "think" about my articles before I do them. So I like to do my interviews and research, and then have at least a week or two (preferably more) for everything to come together in my mind before I write the article. If my deadline is far enough into the future that I can do my work this way, I can think through and plan the whole article several times, and then when I sit down to do the actual writing it doesn't take me very long at all. (I once wrote a novel in only ten days—after thinking about it and planning it in my mind for over a year.) Maybe this method will work for you too. Give it a try.

If procrastination is not the problem, and you do work hard and efficiently but simply cannot get the work done in a reasonable amount of time, maybe you're trying to do articles that are too complicated for your level of experience. I'm sure, for example, that any competent writer could do a good article covering the explanations of the oddest theories in modern quantum physics—and I don't know about you, but an article like that would take me a couple of years to do, even if I really wanted to do it. It's just so far beyond me and what I know that I wouldn't have a chance of meeting a three-month deadline. If you think this may be your problem, try suggesting ideas that are easier to do—at least until you better develop your research and interviewing skills.

Writing is also always easier and goes faster when you feel good (and awake)—maybe you simply need to change your working hours. If you've been working at night, try working in the morning or vice versa.

Or maybe you've been trying to do your articles in just a couple of long sittings. Try breaking them up into more manageable chunks. Work only a half hour for each of fourteen days rather than trying to squeeze the whole job into a day or two.

I think that the solution to your time problem is simply to make yourself start earlier—don't wait until just a few days before your article is due. When you have a lot of time you can work better. And you'll find that your articles turn out better too.

If You've Enjoyed

THE NO-BULL GUIDE TO GETTING PUBLISHED AND MAKING IT AS A WRITER

. . . why not share it with your friends?

As a reader of this book you may order additional copies to give to your friends as gifts at a very special reduced price.

Since you would like to be a successful writer, you probably know other people who have this same desire. A gift of a copy of this book will be remembered and appreciated for years to come.

The regular price is $10.00 per copy, but your special reduced price is only $24.00 for three copies. Please use the order form on the last page to get this special price.

PROFESSIONAL
WRITING AND EDITING SERVICES

from Michelle West

The author of this book is happy to offer comprehensive writing and editing services to help you get started or move further ahead in the fields of writing or publishing.

The most popular service is the manuscript evaluation. For only $100 Ms. West will read up to four chapters of your book or four articles (depending on length) and give you a complete analysis of your project and your writing skills. In a several-page written report she will cover the saleability of your ideas, what is right and wrong with your writing, where you can improve (if applicable), what (if anything) is needed to make your book or articles ready to market or publish and more. Your report will cover everything that you need to know about your manuscript or project.

Other services available include:

* Ghostwriting your books, articles and brochures.
* Polishing or editing your manuscripts—books or articles.
* Complete organization and rewriting of manuscripts.
* Complete production of your book from start to finish.
* Complete newsletter production.
* Consulting on magazine writing or production.
* Consulting on book publishing and production.

A brochure is available listing all available services and fees.

The office is fully computerized, and she can supply you with camera-ready computer typeset copy (letter-quality daisy wheel), professionally typeset camera-ready copy, or send you the floppy disk so that you can have the typesetting done locally at the lowest possible cost.

To obtain a free brochure listing all services and fees, please send a long SASE to: Michelle West, c/o Winslow Publishing, Box 413, Station Z, Toronto, Ontario M5N 2Z5 Canada

OTHER BOOKS AVAILABLE FROM WINSLOW PUBLISHING

An Introduction To Self-Publishing With Resource List by Carolyn Winslow—This booklet explains how Winslow Publishing was started and became a very successful small press. If you're thinking about starting a small publishing company, this book will give you the basics. It is free to the readers of this book—just send three loose stamps (American or Canadian) for postage.

The Complete Guide To Companion Advertising by Carolyn Winslow— A comprehensive guide to finding friends and lovers through newspaper and magazine companion ad columns. These ads are growing in popularity primarily because people are too busy these days to spend the time to meet others in the traditional ways. With only one ad you can reach thousands —or maybe millions—of possible partners. Those whose heart you have touched with your ad will respond. Learn all of the secrets with this book.

Mind Over Money —If you've long dreamed of having your own business, this book is just what the doctor ordered. It not only explains in detail how to succeed in a fabulous unique enterprise, but also gives you the extra enthusiasm and motivation you need to really achieve something for yourself. Buying this book entitles you to one year's free consultation with the author about your business. Included are business plans for several businesses you can start tomorrow, even if you've never worked for yourself before.

The Unabashed Self-Promoter's Guide: What Every Man, Woman, Child and Organization Needs To Know About Getting Ahead By Exploiting The Media —Using the dozens of promotional and marketing techniques in this widely-acclaimed book, you'll effectively sell your products and services quickly and inexpensively. Whatever you're selling—product, service, organization or yourself—**The Unabashed Self-Promoter's Guide** is your one critical resource. Widely recognized as the definitive book on no-cost/low-cost marketing strategies, it's must reading for anyone with limited resources and the pressing need to reach your buyers. Don't spend another nickel on advertising until you've learned the profit-making techniques of this shrewd, humorous, ingenious book.

The Consultant's Kit: Establishing And Operating Your Successful Consulting Business —Thousands and thousands of people are now using this book to build successful part-time and full-time consulting businesses in any field. Here in one fast-moving easy-to-read volume is just what you need to know to start profiting from the knowledge and expertise you already have. You'll find out if you're equipped to succeed in consulting, how to position yourself for success, what you need to know to begin marketing yourself successfully, how to deal with client prospects, information on contracts and fees, making the best use of independent contractors, building a network of sustaining clients, and much, much more. You won't find a more complete book on this subject.

Money Talks: The Complete Guide To Creating A Profitable Workshop Or Seminar In Any Field —If you know something and can open your mouth, this book's for you! Now learn *exactly* what you need to know to make money on North America's multi-billion dollar talk circuit. Regarded as the "bible" for those wanting to prosper through any kind of talk program, **Money Talks** contains just what you need to know so you can promote yourself, get new clients, and make money through talk. A huge hard-hitting thorough guide for anyone who wants to venture into the talk-for-money business—or who wants to do better in it.

Tricks Of The Trade: The Complete Guide To Succeeding In The Advice Business —This new book takes up where **The Consultant's Kit** leaves off. This step-by-step plan is for people who already have some experience in advising, who want to build a more lucrative practice, or who are looking for those hard-to-discover facts which insure success in any field. This information-rich book is chock full of material impossible to find anywhere else—material about effectively targeting client prospects, writing winning proposals, working with clients to insure success on the job, leveraging your successes to other people and organizations who want to replicate them, becoming an up-to-date computer-assisted advisor, how to diversify and create your 10-Step Mobile Mini-Conglomerate to make maximum profit from what you know and can do so that you'll make money every day of your life. Millions of North Americans are succeeding in the advice business. With **Tricks Of The Trade** you can be one of them.

How To Make Money Writing And Selling Simple Information —Make money writing books, reports and newsletters—how-to material of every kind for the giant mail order booktrade. Turn your ideas into informative manuscripts, market them, run inexpensive ads, and get dealers to help you sell your wares. Full of valuable professional pointers.

How To Publish Your Own Book Successfully —Why sell books that others have produced when you can easily and inexpensively produce your own books and keep all of the profits? This is a basic guide to starting up your own small press, and will answer all of your questions. Writing and printing a book is only one part of being a successful publisher—selling your book is all important. There's a lot of money to be made in the information-by-mail industry—why not grab a part of it now?

Formaides For Successful Book Publishing —Save time, money and hassles in producing and promoting your books. This is a complete collection of forms, records, sample letters and procedures to help you insure your success as an independent publisher.

How To Sell Books By Mail —Learn how to plan a complete campaign, choose the right books, write powerful advertising, get the most from your advertising dollars, select good mailing lists, and lots more. Includes a list of hundreds of wholesale book dealers you can buy from if you don't want to publish your own books.

How To Get Rich In Mail Order —This book was written by one of the most famous and successful publishers and book-sellers of all time, and covers every aspect of the mail order industry. If you want to sell books or other products through the mail, this guide will show you everything you need to know to be a smashing success. 336 pages, 8 1/2" by 11", 200 illustrations, crammed with valuable information.

How To Start Making Money In A Business Of Your Own—420 pages of easy-to-understand information that covers everything you need to know to start and succeed in your own business. Included are over 102 moneymaking business opportunities, many of which can be started from scratch with little or no investment. You'll learn about many successful businesses, including franchising, construction, self-publishing, mail order, retailing, cashing in on your inventions, ways to make money by moonlighting and lots more.

Making $500,000 A Year In Mail Order —If you've ever dreamed of having your mailbox crammed with thousands of envelopes, each containing a check with your name on it, working any hours you want, whenever you want, and being able to afford the greatest pleasures that life has to offer, then this book can help you make those dreams a reality. Full of helpful, easy-to-use information written by a mail order professional, this book will show you how to market books through the mail as well as other products. Includes confidential advertising results. If you plan to publish books or other information, mail order is the absolutely best way to reach new customers.

500 Moneymaking Mail Order Ideas —There is a market everywhere for products and services that will save the customer money or make money for him. Find a need and fill it—and watch your profits come rolling in. If you've wanted to start a mail order business, but weren't sure what direction you should take, then dip into this book for over 500 great ideas. Don't wait until tomorrow!

How To Achieve Total Success —Nothing is impossible if you really believe in yourself. This book will show you how to set and achieve powerful goals, the dynamics of affirmations that will deliver the results you desire, effective use of Creative Visualization, the secret power of a Success Covenant, and wealth-building techniques that will create riches for you. This is one of the most positive books you'll ever read—learn how to get "high" on life and enjoy every good and every happiness in your business and your relationships.

Please see the next page for order form

ORDER FORM

Winslow Publishing
Box 413, Station Z
Toronto, ON M5N 2Z5 Canada
(416) 789-4733

Please send me the following books:

QUANTITY
____ The No-Bull Guide To Getting Published And Making It As A Writer
—$10.00 each, $24.00 for three
____ An Introduction To Self-Publishing—3 loose stamps
____ The Complete Guide To Companion Advertising—$5.00
____ Mind Over Money—$15.00
____ The Unabashed Self-Promoter's Guide—$31.50
____ The Consultant's Kit—$31.50
____ Money Talks—$31.50
____ Tricks Of The Trade—$31.50
____ How To Make Money Writing And Selling Simple Information—$15.00
____ How To Publish Your Own Book Successfully—$10.00
____ Formaides For Successful Book Publishing—$10.00
____ How To Sell Books By Mail—$10.00
____ How To Get Rich In Mail Order—$15.00
____ How To Start Making Money In A Business Of Your Own—$15.00
____ Making $500,000 A Year In Mail Order—$15.00
____ 500 Moneymaking Mail Order Ideas—$10.00
____ How To Achieve Total Success—$15.00

____ Total number of books ordered
Please add Shipping (see below)   * _____
Total   * _____

Shipping: Please add $1.50 postage and handling for the first book, $.50 for each additional book

All amounts are payable in U.S. dollars. Check, Money Order, Visa or Mastercard welcome.

Customers from the U.S. pay no customs duty or taxes on these books

Name _____

Address _____

_____

Visa or Mastercard Number _____

Expiry Date _____ Signature _____

147

ORDER FORM

Winslow Publishing
Box 413, Station Z
Toronto, ON M5N 2Z5 Canada
(416) 789-4733

Please send me the following books:

QUANTITY

____ The No-Bull Guide To Getting Published And Making It As A Writer
—$10.00 each, $24.00 for three
____ An Introduction To Self-Publishing—3 loose stamps
____ The Complete Guide To Companion Advertising—$5.00
____ Mind Over Money—$15.00
____ The Unabashed Self-Promoter's Guide—$31.50
____ The Consultant's Kit—$31.50
____ Money Talks—$31.50
____ Tricks Of The Trade—$31.50
____ How To Make Money Writing And Selling Simple Information—$15.00
____ How To Publish Your Own Book Successfully—$10.00
____ Formaides For Successful Book Publishing—$10.00
____ How To Sell Books By Mail—$10.00
____ How To Get Rich In Mail Order—$15.00
____ How To Start Making Money In A Business Of Your Own—$15.00
____ Making $500,000 A Year In Mail Order—$15.00
____ 500 Moneymaking Mail Order Ideas—$10.00
____ How To Achieve Total Success—$15.00

____ Total number of books ordered
Please add Shipping (see below)   *   _____
Total   *   _____

Shipping: Please add $1.50 postage and handling for the first book, $.50 for each additional book.

All amounts are payable in U.S. dollars. Check, Money Order, Visa or Mastercard welcome.

Customers from the U.S. pay no customs duty or taxes on these books

Name _____

Address _____

_____

Visa or Mastercard Number _____

Expiry Date _____ Signature _____

ORDER FORM

Winslow Publishing
Box 413, Station Z
Toronto, ON M5N 2Z5 Canada
(416) 789-4733

Please send me the following books:

QUANTITY
____ The No-Bull Guide To Getting Published And Making It As A Writer
    —$10.00 each, $24.00 for three
____ An Introduction To Self-Publishing—3 loose stamps
____ The Complete Guide To Companion Advertising—$5.00
____ Mind Over Money—$15.00
____ The Unabashed Self-Promoter's Guide—$31.50
____ The Consultant's Kit—$31.50
____ Money Talks—$31.50
____ Tricks Of The Trade—$31.50
____ How To Make Money Writing And Selling Simple Information—$15.00
____ How To Publish Your Own Book Successfully—$10.00
____ Formaides For Successful Book Publishing—$10.00
____ How To Sell Books By Mail—$10.00
____ How To Get Rich In Mail Order—$15.00
____ How To Start Making Money In A Business Of Your Own—$15.00
____ Making $500,000 A Year In Mail Order—$15.00
____ 500 Moneymaking Mail Order Ideas—$10.00
____ How To Achieve Total Success—$15.00

____ Total number of books ordered
    Please add Shipping (see below) * _____
                    Total * _____

Shipping: Please add $1.50 postage and handling for the first book, $.50 for each additional book

All amounts are payable in U.S. dollars. Check, Money Order, Visa or Mastercard welcome.

Customers from the U.S. pay no customs duty or taxes on these books

Name _____

Address _____

_____

Visa or Mastercard Number _____

Expiry Date _____ Signature _____